Autodesk Fusion 360
Basics Tutorial

Tutorial Books

For resource files, contact us at:

Online.books999@gmail.com

Contents

Contents

Contents

INTRODUCTION

Autodesk Fusion 360 is a web-based modeling program. It is a package of many modules delivering exceptional value to enterprises. It offers a set of tools, which are easy-to-use to design, document, simulate, and manufacture 3D models. Using this software, you can speed up the design process and reduce product development costs.

This book provides a step-by-step approach for users to learn Autodesk Fusion 360. It is aimed at those with no previous experience with Fusion 360. The user will be guided from starting an Autodesk Fusion 360 session to creating parts, assemblies, and drawings. Each chapter has components explained with the help of real-world models.

Scope of this book

This book is written for students and engineers who are interested to learn Autodesk Fusion 360 for designing mechanical components and assemblies, and then create drawings.

This book provides a step-by-step approach for learning Autodesk Fusion 360. The topics include Getting Started with Autodesk Fusion 360, Basic Part Modeling, Creating Assemblies, Creating Drawings, Sketching, Additional Modeling Tools, Top-down assemblies, Dimensions, and Annotations, and Sheet Metal Modeling.

Chapter 1 introduces Autodesk Fusion 360. The user interface and terminology are discussed in this chapter.

Chapter 2 takes you through the creation of your first Fusion 360 model. You create simple parts.

Chapter 3 teaches you to create assemblies. It explains the Top-down and Bottom-up approaches for designing an assembly. You create an assembly using the Bottom-up approach.

Chapter 4 teaches you to create drawings of the models created in the earlier chapters. You will also learn to place exploded views and part list of an assembly.

Chapter 5: In this chapter, you will learn the sketching tools.

Chapter 6: In this chapter, you will learn additional modeling tools to create complex models.

Chapter 7 teaches you to create Top-down assemblies. It also introduces you to create mechanisms by applying joints between the parts.

Chapter 8 teaches you to apply dimensions and annotations to a 2D drawing.

Chapter 9 teaches you to design a sheet metal model.

Contents

Chapter 1: Getting Started with Fusion 360

What is Fusion 360?

Autodesk Fusion 360 is a web and cloud-based modeling application. Some of the key features of Fusion 360 are:

- Web and cloud-based
- It supports Parametric and Direct Modeling
- It can be accessed from anywhere
- It helps you to collaborate with a team
- Simple user-interface
- It supports Free-form modeling
- It allows you to work on models created in other CAD applications
- It helps you to 3D print a model or generates toolpaths using Manufacture Workspace.
- It helps you to perform a Design study using the Simulation feature.
- It is updated very frequently, unlike other CAD programs.

This tutorial book brings in the most commonly used features of Autodesk Fusion 360. In this chapter, you will learn about the Autodesk Fusion 360 user interface and some of its most frequently used features. In Autodesk Fusion 360, you create 3D parts and use them to create 2D drawings and 3D assemblies.

Fusion 360 is Feature Based. Features are shapes that are combined to build a part. You can modify these shapes individually.

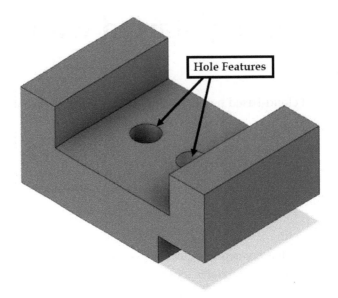

Hole Features

Most of the features are sketch-based. A sketch is a 2D profile and can be extruded, revolved, or swept along a path to create features.

Autodesk Fusion 360 is parametric in nature. You can specify standard parameters between the elements. Changing these parameters changes the size and shape of the part. For example, see the design of the flange before and after modifying the parameters of its features.

Starting Autodesk Fusion 360

- Click the Windows icon on the taskbar.
- Click **A** > **Autodesk** > **Autodesk Fusion 360**.

Notice these essential features of the Fusion 360 window.

1. Toolbar
2. Application Bar
3. Browser

4. Navigation Bar
5. Timeline
6. ViewCube

User Interface

Various components of the user interface are discussed next.

Toolbar

The toolbar is located at the top of the window. The toolbar consists of various tabs. Each tab has tools that are arranged on panels. You can select the required tool from a panel. By default, only a few tools are displayed on a panel. You need to click the down arrow shown on the panel to access more tools.

The set of tools displayed on the Toolbar depends on the Workspace, which is currently active. You can change the workspace by using the **Change Workspace** drop-down displayed on the left side. Click on this drop-down and select the required workspace; a set of tools related to the chosen workspace appear on the toolbar. The following sections explain the various workspaces available in Autodesk Fusion 360.

The Design Workspace

The Design workspace is used to design the 3D geometry. The Toolbar in this workspace has four different tabs. The **Solid** tab consists of the tools to create sketches, 3D features, planes, and assemblies.

The **Sketch** contextual tab appears when you activate the sketch mode. The tools on this contextual tab are used to create and modify sketches.

The **Surface** tab consists of the tools to create and modify surfaces. The remaining tools on this toolbar are the same as that available on the Solid tab of the toolbar.

The tools on the **Sheet Metal** tab are used to create sheet metal components.

The **Tools** tab has tools to inspect and 3D print.

The Render Workspace

The Toolbar in this workspace contains the tools to create photorealistic images and videos.

The Animation Workspace

The Toolbar in this workspace contains the tools to create the exploded views of an assembly. It also has the tools to create an animation of an assembly.

The Simulation Workspace

The Toolbar in this workspace contains the tools to perform engineering analysis of the components and assemblies.

The Manufacture Workspace

The Toolbar in this workspace contains the tools to generate toolpaths for manufacturing operations such as milling, drilling, turning, and so on.

The Drawing Workspace

In the Drawing workspace, you can create print-ready drawings of a 3D model. The Toolbar in this workspace contains the tools to create 2D drawings.

File Menu

This appears when you click on the **File** icon located at the top left corner. This menu contains the options to create a design, import design, print, export, manage, save, and so on.

Application Bar

The Application bar is available at the top left corner of the window. It contains the **File** menu, **Save**, **Undo**, and **Redo** icons. You can use the **Show Data Panel** (grid) icon to view the data panel.

Browser

The Browser is located on the left side of the window. It contains the **Document Settings**, **Named Views**, and **Origin** folder. In addition to that, the bodies, components, sketches, and construction elements are grouped in folders. You can show or hide them using the visibility icons located next to them.

Timeline

The Timeline is displayed at the bottom of the window. It shows the operations carried in an Autodesk Fusion 360 file. The Timeline is a crucial feature in making Autodesk Fusion 360 a parametric modeling software. You can edit a sketch, feature, or construction element by merely double-clicking on them in the Timeline. Click the Play button to view the sequence in which the model was created. Click and drag the Play Marker before a feature; the feature is suppressed.

Navigation Bar

The Navigation Bar is located at the bottom of the graphics window above the Timeline. It contains the tools to zoom, rotate, pan, or look at the face of the model. You can also access the display settings, grid and snap settings, and viewport settings.

View Cube

It is located at the top right corner of the graphics window. It is used to set the view orientation of the model.

Press and hold the left mouse button on the corner, and then drag

Shortcut and Marking Menus

When you click the right mouse button, a shortcut menu along with a marking menu appears. A shortcut menu contains some essential options.

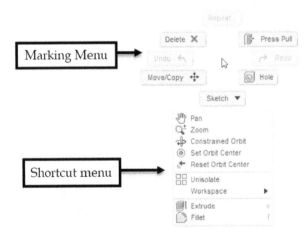

The marking menu contains some essential tools in a radial fashion. It allows you to access the tools quickly.

Dialogs

When you activate any tool in Autodesk Fusion 360, the dialog related to it appears. It consists of various options, which help you to complete the operation. The following figure shows the components of the dialog.

Customizing the Toolbar

By default, not all tools are displayed on the Toolbar. However, you can show them on the panels of the Toolbar. To do this, click the down arrow displayed at the bottom of the panel. Next, place the pointer on the tool to be displayed on the panel. Click on the three dots displayed next to the tool, and then select Pin to Toolbar; the tool will be pinned to the Toolbar.

If you want to reset the panel, then right click on it and select **Reset Panel Customization**.

The Quick Setup dialog

The **Quick Setup** dialog helps you to specify the default units and navigation controls. Also, you can start learning using the guided tutorials. This book uses **Inches** to create models, so it is advised to set the **Default Units** to **in**. You can specify the navigation controls based on any other CAD application.

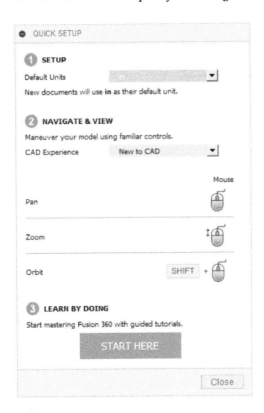

Chapter 2: Part Modeling Basics

This chapter takes you through the creation of your first Fusion 360 model. You create simple parts:

In this chapter, you will:

- Create Sketches
- Create a base feature
- Add another feature to it
- Create revolved features
- Create cylindrical features
- Create box features
- Apply draft

TUTORIAL 1

This tutorial takes you through the creation of your first Fusion 360 model. You will create the Disc of an Oldham coupling:

Creating a New Project

1. Start **Autodesk Fusion 360** by double-clicking the **Autodesk Fusion 360** icon on your desktop.
2. To create a new project, click the **Show Data Panel** button located at the top left corner of the window.

3. Click the **Return to project list** button.

4. Click the **New Project** button.

5. Type **Oldham Coupling** and press Enter.

6. Click the **Close Data Panel** button.

7. Click the **Help** icon located on the top right corner of the window, and then select **Quick Setup**.
8. On the **Quick Setup** dialog, select **Default Units > in**.
9. Select **CAD Experience > New to CAD**.
10. Click **Close** on the **Quick Setup** dialog.

Starting a Sketch

1. To start a new sketch, click **Solid** tab **> Create panel > Create Sketch** on the Toolbar.

2. Click on the **XZ Plane**. The sketch starts.

The first feature is an extruded feature from a sketched circular profile. You will begin by sketching the circle.

3. On the Toolbar, click the **Sketch** contextual tab **> Create** panel **> Circle > Center Diameter Circle**.

4. Move the cursor to the sketch origin located at the center of the graphics window, and then click on it.
5. Drag the cursor up to a random location, and then click to create a circle.

6. Press **ESC** to deactivate the tool.

Adding Dimensions

In this section, you will specify the size of the sketched circle by adding dimensions. As you add dimensions, the sketch can attain any one of the following states:

Fully Constrained sketch: In a fully constrained sketch, the positions of all the entities are fully described by dimensions, constraints, or both. In a fully constrained sketch, all the entities are black in color.

Under Constrained sketch: Additional dimensions, constraints, or both are needed to specify the geometry completely. In this state, you can drag under constrained sketch entities to modify the sketch. An under constrained sketch entity is in blue color.

If you add any more dimensions to a fully constrained sketch, a message box will appear, showing that dimension over constraints the sketch. Also, it prompts you to convert the dimension into a driven dimension. Click **Ok** to change the unwanted dimension into a driven dimension.

1. On the Toolbar, click **Sketch** contextual tab > **Create** panel > **Sketch Dimension**.

(or)

Right click on the graphics window, and then place the pointer on the **Sketch** option. Next, select **Sketch Dimension**.

2. Select the circle, move the pointer, and click; a value box appears.
3. Enter **4** in the value box and press Enter.
4. Press **Esc** to deactivate the **Sketch Dimension** tool.

You can also create dimensions while creating sketch objects. To do this, enter the dimension values in the boxes displayed while sketching.

5. To display the entire circle at full size and to center it in the graphics area, click **Zoom Window > Fit** 🔍 on the **Navigation Bar**.

6. Click **Finish Sketch** on the Toolbar.

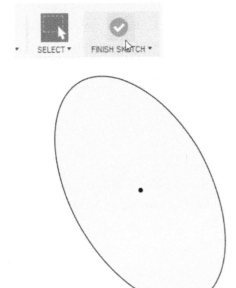

Creating the Base Feature

The first feature in any part is called a base feature. You now create this feature by extruding the sketched circle.

1. On the Toolbar, click the **Solid** tab **> Create** panel **> Extrude.**

2. Click on the region enclosed by the sketch.
3. Type-in 0.4 in the **Distance** box available on the **Extrude** dialog.
4. Select **Direction > One Side** ⟫ on the **Extrude** dialog.
5. Click **OK** on the **Extrude** dialog to create the extrusion.

Notice the new feature, **Extrude 1**, in the **Timeline**.

To magnify a model in the graphics area, you can use the zoom tools available on the **Navigation Bar**.

Click **Fit** to display the full part size in the current window.

Click **Zoom Window**, and then drag the pointer to create a rectangle; the area in the rectangle zooms to fill the window.

Click **Zoom**, and then drag the pointer. Dragging up zooms out; dragging down zooms in.

To display the part in different rendering modes, select the options in the **Visual Style** menu on the **Display Settings** drop-down of the Navigation Bar.

Shaded

Shaded with Hidden Edges

Shaded with Visible Edges Only

Wireframe

Wireframe with Hidden Edges

Wireframe with Visible Edges Only

The default display mode for parts and assemblies is **Shaded with Visible Edges Only**. You may change the display mode whenever you want.

Adding an Extruded Feature

To create additional features on the part, you need to draw sketches on the model faces or planes, and then extrude them.

1. On the Toolbar, click the **Solid** tab > **Create** panel > **Create Sketch**.
2. Click on the front face of the part.

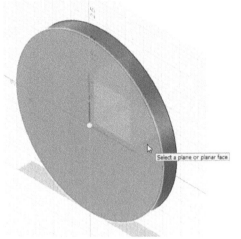

3. Click the **Sketch** contextual tab > **Create** panel > **Line** on the Toolbar.

4. Click on the circular edge to specify the first point of the line.

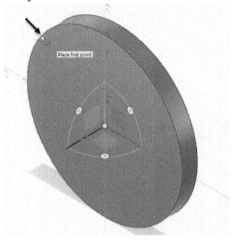

5. Move the cursor towards the right.
6. Click on the other side of the circular edge; a line is drawn.

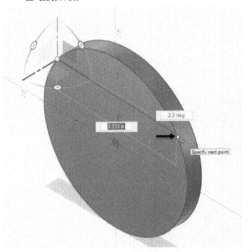

7. Draw another line below the previous line.

8. On the **Sketch** contextual tab of the Toolbar, click **Constraints** panel **> Horizontal/Vertical**.

9. Select the two lines to make them horizontal.

10. On the **Sketch** contextual tab of the Toolbar, click **Constraints > Equal** ═ .

11. Select the two horizontal lines to make them equal in length.

12. Click **Sketch Dimension** ├─┤ on the **Create** panel of the **Sketch** contextual tab Toolbar.

13. Select the two horizontal lines.

14. Move the cursor toward the right and click to locate the dimension; the value box appears.

15. Enter **0.472** in the value box and press Enter.

16. Click **Finish Sketch** on the toolbar.

17. On the Toolbar, click the **Solid** tab **> Create** panel **> Extrude**.

18. Click on the region bounded by the two horizontal lines.

19. Enter **0.4** in the **Distance** box on the **Extrude** dialog.

20. On the **Extrude** dialog, click **Direction > One Side.**

21. Select **Operation > Join**, and then **OK** to create the extrusion.

By default, the ground shadows and ambient occlusion are displayed on the model. However, you can turn off them by clicking **Navigation Bar > Display Settings > Effects** menu, and then unchecking the **Ground Shadows** and **Ambient Occlusion** options.

*You can reuse the sketch of an already existing feature. To do this, expand the **Sketches** folder in the Browser, and then click on the visibility icon located next to the sketch. You will notice that the sketch is visible in the graphics window. You can also hide the sketch by again clicking on the visibility icon next to the sketch.*

Adding another Extruded Feature

1. Click **Orbit > Free Orbit** on the **Navigation Bar.**

2. Press and hold the left mouse button and drag the pointer to rotate the model.
3. Release the mouse button when the back face of the part is visible.

4. Right click and select **OK.**

5. Click **Create Sketch** on the **Create** panel of the **Solid** tab of the Toolbar.
6. Click on the back face of the part.
7. Click the **Look at** icon on the Navigation Bar.

8. Select the back face of the part.
9. Click the **Sketch** tab > **Create** panel > **Line**.
10. Draw two lines, as shown below (refer to the **Adding an Extruded Feature** section to know how to draw lines). Make sure that the endpoints of the lines are coincident with the circular edge. Follow the next two steps, if they are not coincident.

11. On the **Sketch** contextual tab of the Toolbar, click **Constraints > Coincident**. Next, select the endpoint of the line and the circular edge.

12. Likewise, make the other endpoints of the lines coincident with the circular edge.

Skip the above two steps if the endpoints of the lines are coincident with the circular edge.

13. On the **Sketch** contextual tab of the Toolbar, click **Constraints > Horizontal/Vertical** .
14. Select the two lines to make them vertical.
15. On the **Sketch** contextual tab of the Toolbar, click **Sketch** tab **> Constraints** panel **> Equal** .
16. Select the two vertical lines to make them equal.
17. On the **Sketch** contextual tab of the Toolbar, click **Create** panel **> Sketch Dimension** .
18. Select the two vertical lines, move the pointer upward, and then click to position the dimension.
19. Type **0.472** in the value box, and then press Enter.
20. Click **Finish Sketch** on the Toolbar.

21. On the Toolbar, click the **Solid** tab **> Create** panel **> Extrude**.

22. Click inside the region enclosed by two lines.
23. Type **0.4** in the **Distance** box on the **Extrude** dialog.
24. Select **Operation > Join** and click **OK**.

To move the part view, click **Pan** on **Navigation Bar**, and then drag the part to move it in the graphics area.

25. Click on the **Home** icon next to the ViewCube

Saving the Part

1. Click **Save** on the **Application bar**.
2. On the **Save** window, type-in **Disc** in the **Name** box.
3. Click the down arrow button next to the **Location** box.
4. Select **Oldham Coupling** from the **Project** list.
5. Click **Save** to save the file.
6. Click the **Close** icon on the **File** tab.

TUTORIAL 2

In this tutorial, you create a flange by performing the following operations:

- Creating a revolved feature
- Creating cut features
- Adding fillets

Sketching a Revolve Profile

You create the base feature of the flange by revolving a profile around a centerline.

1. Click **Solid** tab > **Create** panel > **Create Sketch** on the Toolbar.

2. Select the YZ plane.

3. Click the **Look At** icon on the **SKETCH PALETTE**.

4. Click **Line** on the **Create** panel.

5. Specify the first point of the line, as shown.

6. Move the pointer horizontally toward left up to a scale value of 2.

7. Click to create a horizontal line of 2 inches.

8. Move the pointer vertically upward.

9. Click when a value of 0.6 is displayed in the dimension attached to the line.

10. Likewise, create the other lines in the sequence, as shown.

11. On the Sketch Palette, click **Options > Construction**.

12. Create a construction line by specifying the start and endpoints, as shown below.

13. Right click and select **OK**.
14. On the **Sketch** contextual tab of the Toolbar, click **Constraints > Coincident** .
15. Select the vertical line and the origin point, as shown.

18. Right click and select **Diameter Dimension**.
19. Move the pointer horizontally toward left and click to place the dimension.
20. Type 1.2 in the value box.
21. Press Enter.

22. Likewise, create two more diameter dimensions, as shown.

16. On the **Sketch** contextual tab of the Toolbar, click **Create** panel **> Sketch Dimension** .
17. Select the construction line and the horizontal line.

27. Move the pointer upward, and click.
28. Type 0.8 and press Enter.

23. With the **Sketch Dimension** tool still active, select the horizontal line, as shown.

24. Move the pointer upward, and click.
25. Type 2 in the value box and press Enter.

26. Select the top horizontal line.

 You can hide all the constraints by unchecking the **Show Constraints** option on the **Sketch Palette**. Likewise, you can display all the constraints by checking the **Show Constraints** option.

29. Click **Finish Sketch** on the Toolbar.

Creating the Revolved Feature

1. On the Toolbar, click the **Solid** tab > **Create** panel > **Revolve**.

2. Click on the region enclosed by the sketch.
3. On the **Revolve** dialog, click the **Select** button next to the **Axis** option.
4. Select the construction line.

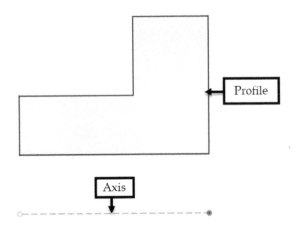

5. Set **Type** to **Full** on the **Revolve** dialog.

6. Click **OK** to create the revolved feature.
7. Click on the **Home** icon next to the ViewCube.

Creating the Cut feature

1. On the Navigation Bar, click **Orbit** > **Constrained Orbit**.

Notice a grey circle with quadrant lines is displayed, as shown.

2. Place the pointer on the right horizontal line.
3. Press and hold the left mouse button and drag the mouse toward left.

4. Release the left mouse button when the back face of the model is visible.
5. Right click and select **OK**.
6. On the Toolbar, click the **Solid** tab > **Create** panel > **Create Sketch** .
7. Click the back face of the part; the sketch starts.

14. Click the **Finish Sketch** button located at the bottom of the Sketch Palette.
15. Press the Ctrl key and click inside the sketch regions, as shown.

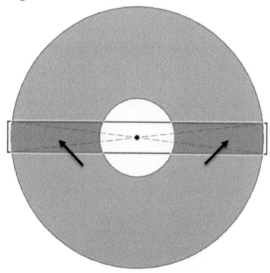

8. Click the **Look At** icon on the **SKETCH PALETTE**.
9. On the Toolbar, click the **Sketch** tab > **Create** panel > **Rectangle** > **Center Rectangle**.
10. Select the origin to define the center point.
11. Move the cursor diagonally toward the right.
12. Enter **0.472** in the vertical dimension box.
13. Press Tab key and enter **4.1** in the horizontal dimension box. Press Enter twice.

16. Right-click and select **Extrude**; the **Extrude** dialog appears.
17. Select **Operation** > **Cut** from the **Extrude** dialog.
18. Enter -0.4 in the **Distance** box.
19. Click **OK** to create the cut feature.

Creating another Cut feature

1. Click the **Home** icon located at the top left corner of the ViewCube.

2. Create a sketch on the front face of the base feature.

- On the Toolbar, click the **Solid** tab > **Create** panel > **Create Sketch**.
- Select the front face of the model.

- Click the **Look At** icon on the **SKETCH PALETTE**.
- On the Toolbar, click the **Sketch** tab > **Create** panel > **Line**.
- Click on the inner circular edge to define the start point, as shown.

- Move the pointer horizontally toward the right, and then click. Notice that the **Horizontal** constraint is applied to the line.
- Move the pointer vertically upward, and then click. Notice that the **Vertical** constraint is applied.
- Move the pointer toward the left and click on the inner circular edge.

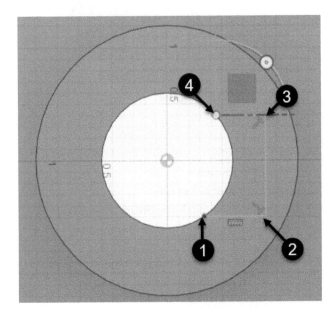

- Right click and select **OK**.
- On the Toolbar, click the **Sketch** tab > **Constraints** panel > **Horizontal/Vertical** ⬚.
- Select the third line to make it horizontal.

- On the Toolbar, click the **Sketch** tab > **Constraints** panel > **Equal**.
- Select the two horizontal lines to make them equal in length.
- Ensure that the endpoints of the horizontal lines coincide with the inner circular edge.
- Apply dimension of 0.236 to the vertical line.
- Apply dimension of 0.118 to the horizontal line.
- Press Esc.

3. Click **Finish Sketch** on the Toolbar.
4. Click **Extrude** on the **Create** panel of the **Solid** tab of the Toolbar.
5. Click on the region enclosed by the three lines and circular edge.

6. Click the **Home** icon next to the ViewCube.
7. On the **Extrude** dialog, select **All** from the **Extent** drop-down.
8. Select **Operation > Cut** from the **Extrude** dialog.
9. Click the **Flip** icon on the **Extrude** dialog, if the arrow on the sketch points towards front.

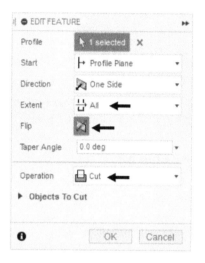

10. Click **OK** to create the cut feature.

Adding a Fillet

1. On the Toolbar, click the **Solid** tab > **Modify** panel > **Fillet**.

2. Click on the inner circular edge.

- Creating a cylindrical feature
- Creating a cut feature

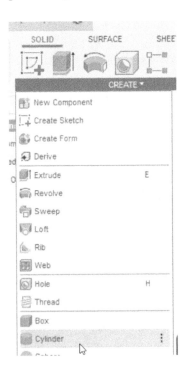

3. On the **Fillet** dialog, select **Type > Constant Radius**.
4. Type 0.2 in the **Radius** box.

5. Click **OK** to add the fillet.

Saving the Part

1. Click **Save** 🖫 on the **Application bar**.
2. On the **Save** window, type-in **Flange** in the **Name** box.
3. Click the down arrow button next to the **Location** box.
4. Select **Oldham Coupling** from the **Project** list.
5. Click **Save** to save the file.
6. Click the **Close** icon on the **File** tab.

TUTORIAL 3

In this tutorial, you create the Shaft by performing the following operations:

Creating the Cylindrical Feature

1. On the Toolbar, click the **Solid** tab > **Create** panel > **Cylinder**.

2. Click on the **XZ** plane to select it; the sketch starts.
3. Click at the origin and move the cursor outward.
4. Enter **1.2** in the box attached to the circle.

- On the Toolbar, click **Sketch** tab **> Create** panel **> Line**.
- Specify the points of the lines in the sequence, as shown.

5. Press the Enter key; the **Cylinder** dialog appears.
6. Enter **4** in the **Height** box.

7. Click **OK** to create the cylinder.

Creating Cut feature

1. Create a sketch on the front face of the base feature.

- On the Toolbar, click **Solid** tab **> Create** panel **> Create Sketch** .

- Select the front face of the cylinder.
- Click the **Look At** icon on the SKETCH PALETTE.

- Right click and select **OK**.

- Make sure that the **Coincident** constraint is applied between the endpoints of the vertical lines and the circular edge.
- On the Toolbar, click the **Sketch** tab > **Constraints** panel > **Equal**.
- Click on the two vertical lines.
- On the Toolbar, click the **Sketch** tab > **Create** panel > **Sketch Dimension**.
- Add dimensions to the sketch.

2. Click **Finish Sketch** on the **Sketch** palette.
3. Click the **Home** icon next to the ViewCube.
4. Click the **Extrude** button on the **Create** panel.
5. Click on the region enclosed by the sketch.
6. Click **Operation > Cut** on the **Extrude** dialog.
7. Set **Distance** to **-2.165**.
8. Click **OK** to create the cut feature.

Saving the Part

1. Click **Save** 🖫 on the **Application bar**.
2. On the **Save** window, type-in **Shaft** in the **Name** box.
3. Click the down arrow button next to the **Location** box.
4. Select **Oldham Coupling** from the **Project** list.
5. Click **Save** to save the file.
6. Click the **Close** icon on the **File** tab.

TUTORIAL 4

In this tutorial, you create a Key by performing the following:

- Creating a Box feature
- Applying draft

Creating a Box

1. On the Toolbar, click the **Solid** tab > **Create** panel > **Box**.

2. Select the XZ plane.
3. Create the sketch, as shown in the figure.

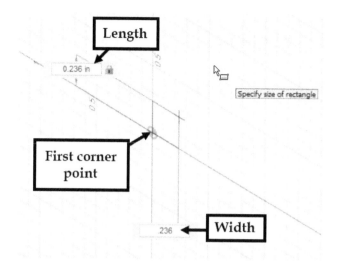

Length

0.236 in

First corner point

Width

236

Specify size of rectangle

4. Press ENTER.
5. Enter **2** in the **Height** box.
6. Click **OK** to create the box.

Applying Draft

1. On the Toolbar, click the **Solid** tab > **Modify** panel > **Draft**.

2. Click the **Select** button next to the **Plane** option.

DRAFT

Plane	Select
Faces	Select
Tangent Chain	☑
Direction	One Side ▾

OK   Cancel

3. Select the front face as the parting plane.

Select parting plane

4. Select the top face as the face to be draft.

Select faces to draft

5. Set **Angle** to **1**.
6. Click the **Flip Direction** button on the **Draft** dialog.

7. Click **OK** to create the draft.

Saving the Part

1. Click **Save** 🖫 on the **Application bar**.

2. On the **Save** window, type-in **Key** in the **Name** box.

3. Click **Save** to save the file.

4. Click the **Close** icon on the File tab.

Chapter 3: Assembly Basics

In this chapter, you will:

- Add Components to assembly
- Apply constraints between components
- Check Degrees of Freedom
- Check Interference
- Create an exploded view of the assembly

TUTORIAL 1

This tutorial takes you through the creation of your first assembly. You create the Oldham coupling assembly:

PARTS LIST		
ITEM	PART NUMBER	QTY
1	Disc	1
2	Flange	2
3	Shaft	2
4	Key	2

There are two ways of creating an assembly model.

- Top-Down Approach
- Bottom-Up Approach

Top-Down Approach

The assembly file is created first, and components are created in that file.

Bottom-Up Approach

The components are created first and then added to the assembly file. In this tutorial, you will create the assembly using this approach.

Inserting the Base Component

You need to save the design before inserting a component into it.

1. On the Application Bar, click the **Save** icon.
2. Type **Flange assembly** in the **Name** box on the **Save** dialog.
   . Click **Save**.
   To insert the base component, click the **Show Data Panel** icon.

5. Right click on the **Flange** file in the Data panel, and then select **Insert into Current Design**.

6. Click **OK** on the **Move/Copy** dialog.
7. In the Browser, right click on the **Flange**, and then select **Ground**; the component is fixed, and it is unmovable.

Adding the second component

1. To insert the second component, right-click on the **Shaft** in the **Data** panel, and then select **Insert into Current Design**.

2. Click and drag the Y-axis of the **Move** tool towards left.

3. Click **OK** on the **Move/Copy** dialog.
4. Close the **Data** panel.

Assembling the Components

After inserting the components into the design, you need to assemble them together. Autodesk Fusion 360 provides you with the **Joint** tool to assemble the components and establish real-life movements between them.

1. On the Toolbar, click **Solid** tab > **Assembly** panel > **Joint**.

2. On the **Joint** dialog, click the **Motion** tab, and then select **Type > Rigid**.

3. Select **Mode > Simple** from the **Component 1** section.
4. Click the **Select** button next to the **Snap** option.

5. Select the circular edge of the shaft, as shown.

6. Select the circular edge on the backside of the flange, as shown.

7. Click the **Flip** icon on the **Joint** dialog.
8. Type **270** in the **Angle** box; the shaft is rotated by the specified angle.
9. Type **-0.4** in the **Offset Z** box; the shaft is offset by the specified distance. Also, the flat face of the shaft is aligned with the planar face of the cut feature, as shown.

10. Click **OK** on the **Joint** dialog.

Adding the Third Component

1. Click the **Show Data Panel** icon on the top left corner of the window.
2. On the **Data** panel, right click on **Key** and select **Insert into Current Design**.
3. Click and drag the arrow, pointing toward the right.

4. Click **OK** on the **Move/Copy** dialog.

5. Close the **Data** panel.
6. On the **Solid** tab of the Toolbar, click **Assemble > Joint**.
7. On the **Joint** dialog, click the **Motion** tab, and then select **Type > Rigid**.
8. Move the pointer onto the side face of the key.
9. Press and hold the left mouse button to display a dialog.
10. Move the pointer over the faces displayed on the dialog until the bottom face of the key is highlighted.
11. Select the highlighted face from the dialog.

14. Select the midpoint of the edge, as shown.

12. Select the midpoint of the lower front edge of the key to define the pivot point.

15. On the **Joint** dialog, type **180** in the **Angle** box.
16. Click **OK**.

13. Select the flat face of the cut feature of the shaft.

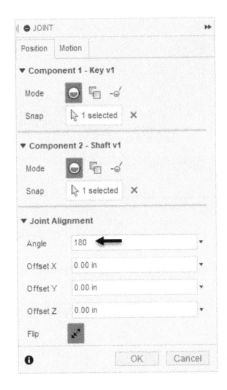

The key is inserted in the cut feature of the shaft.

17. Click **Save** 🖫 on the **Application bar**.
18. Click **OK** on the **Version Description** dialog.
19. Click the **Close** icon on the File tab.

Creating the Main Assembly

When you close a file, a new file is opened automatically.

1. On the Application Bar, click the **Save** icon.

2. Type **Oldham Coupling** in the **Name** box on the **Save** dialog.
3. Click **Save**.
4. To insert the base component, click the **Show Data Panel** icon.
5. Right click on the **Disc** file in the **Data** panel, and then select **Insert into Current Design**.
6. Click **OK** on the **Move/Copy** dialog.
7. In the Browser, right click on the **Disc**, and then select **Ground**.

Placing the Sub-assembly

1. To insert the sub-assembly, right click on the **Flange assembly** file in the **Data** panel, and then select **Insert into Current Design**; the Flange assembly is inserted into the design.
2. Click and drag the arrow displayed in the front direction; the flange assembly is moved.

3. Click **OK** on the **Move/Copy** dialog.

Adding Joints

1. Click **Joint** 🔗 on the **Assemble** panel of the **Solid** tab of the Toolbar.

2. Click the **Motion** tab, and then select **Type >
   Rigid** on the **Joint** dialog.
3. Place the pointer on the flat face of the cut
   feature.
4. Click on the flat face when the pivot point is
   displayed on the midpoint of the edge, as
   shown.

The midpoint of the edge is selected as the pivot
point.

5. Click **Orbit > Free Orbit** on the Navigation Bar.
6. Press and hold the left mouse button and drag
   the pointer upward, as shown.

7. Press and hold the left mouse button on the
   front face of the Disc; a dialog pops up.
8. Select the bottom face of the extruded feature
   from the dialog.

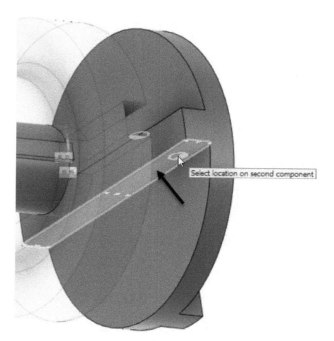

9. Select the midpoint of the edge to define the
   pivot point, as shown.

10. Type **0** in the **Angle** box.
11. Click **OK**.

Placing the second instance of the Sub-assembly

1. In the Browser, right click on the **Flange assembly**, and then select **Copy**.
2. Right click on the graphics window, and then select **Paste**.
3. Click and drag the arrow pointing in the backward direction, as shown.

4. Click on the Rotate handle displayed along the Y-axis.
5. Type 180 in the **Angle** box displayed in the graphics window, and then press Enter.

6. Click on the Rotate handle displayed along the Z-axis.
7. Type 90 in the **Angle** box displayed in the graphics window, and then press Enter.

8. Right click and select **OK**.

9. Click **Joint** on the **Assemble** panel on the **Solid** tab of the Toolbar.
10. Click the **Motion** tab, and then select **Type > Rigid** on the **Joint** dialog.
11. Press and hold the left mouse button on the upper portion of the front face of the flange assembly.
12. Select the side face of the cut feature, as shown.

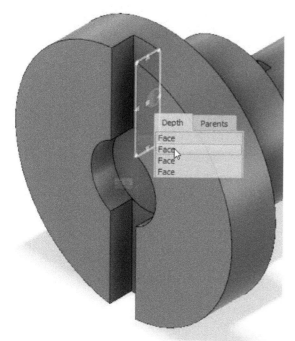

13. Select the midpoint of the top edge to define the pivot point.

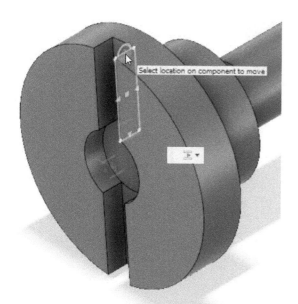

14. Place the pointer on the top portion of the side face of the **Disc**.
15. Click when the pivot point appears on the midpoint of the top edge.

16. Click **OK**.

17. Click **Save** on the Application Bar.
18. Click **OK**.

TUTORIAL 2

In this tutorial, you create the exploded view of the assembly:

Starting a New Animation

1. Open the **Oldham Coupling** file, if not already opened.

2. On the Toolbar, click **Change Workspace** drop-down > **ANIMATION**.

The ANIMATION Workspace appears, as shown.

Creating a Storyboard Animation

1. In the ANIMATION TIMELINE, right-click on the **Storyboard1** tab and select **Rename**.

2. Type **Explosion** and press **Enter**.

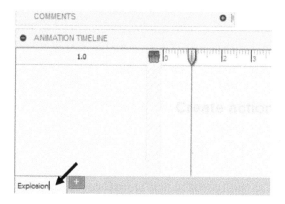

Before creating an exploded view, you need to take a look at the **Storyboard** displayed at the bottom of the window. The **Storyboard** has the **Scratch Zone** located on the left side of the timeline.

Auto Explode Components

1. In the Browser, click the **Components** node to select all the components of the assembly.

2. Click the **Auto Explode: All Levels** button on the **Transform** panel of the Toolbar. A mini toolbar appears, as shown.

3. Adjust the explosion distance using the **Explosion Scale** dragger.
4. Click the **Trail Line Visibility** icon on the Mini toolbar.

5. Click **OK** ✔ on the mini toolbar to explode the components.

6. Select **Components** from the Browser.
7. On the Toolbar, click **Transform > Restore Home**.

The components are restored to their original position.

45

8. Click the **Fullscreen** icon located at the bottom of the storyboard; the model is displayed in the full-screen window.

9. Click the **Play Current Storyboard** icon; the explosion is played.

10. Click the **Normal Mode** icon located at the bottom right corner.

Publishing the Animation Video

1. On the Toolbar, click **Publish** panel > **Publish Video** .
2. On the **Video Options** dialog, select the **Current Storyboard** option from the **Video Scope** drop-down.
3. On the **Video Options** dialog, select the **Current Document Window Size** option from the **Video Resolution** section.
4. Click **OK**.
5. Check the **Save to Computer** option, and then click the folder icon.
6. Specify the file location on the computer.
7. Type Auto_explode in the **File name** box.
8. Set the Save as type to AVI (*.avi).
9. Click **Save** twice.

TUTORIAL 3

In this tutorial, you will explode the components of the assembly manually.

Exploding the Components Manually

1. On the Toolbar, click **Storyboard > New Storyboard**.

2. On the **New Storyboard** dialog, select **Storyboard Type > Clean**.
3. Click **OK**.
4. Click the Minimize icon on the ANIMATION TIMELINE.

5. On the Toolbar, click **Transform > Manual Explode**.

6. Select the **Shaft** from the graphics window, as shown.
7. Click on the arrow pointing in the Z-axis, as shown.

8. Click the **Trail Line Visibility** icon on the mini toolbar.
9. Click and drag the **Explosion Scale** dragger and position it in the middle.

10. Click **OK**.
11. Click **Fit** on the **Navigation Bar**.

12. Likewise, explode the remaining components, as shown.

13. Click the Maximize icon on the ANIMATION TIMELINE.

Notice that the actions are recorded on the timeline.

Right click on any one of the actions and notice the different options in the Shortcut menu.

You can perform various operations on an action such as changing its duration, editing, changing the start/end, or deleting.

14. Publish the animation to a video file (refer to **Publishing the Animation Video** section in Tutorial 2).
15. Save and close the Assembly file.

Chapter 4: Creating Drawings

In this chapter, you will generate 2D drawings of the parts and assemblies.

In this chapter, you will:

- Insert standard views of a part model
- Create centerlines and centermarks
- Retrieve model dimensions
- Add additional dimensions and annotations
- Insert exploded view of the assembly
- Insert a bill of materials of the assembly
- Apply balloons to the assembly

TUTORIAL 1

In this tutorial, you will create the drawing of the Flange.ipt file created in the second chapter.

Starting a New Drawing File

1. Click on the **Show Data Panel** icon on the Application Bar.
2. On the **Data** panel, double-click on the **Oldham Coupling** file to open it.

3. Close the **Data** panel.
4. To start a new drawing, click the **File > New Drawing > From Design** on the Application Bar.

Creating Drawings

5. On the **Create Drawing** dialog, uncheck the **Full Assembly** option.
6. Select the Flange from the assembly.

7. Select **Template > From Scratch**.
8. Select **Standard > ASME**.
9. Select **Units > in**.
10. Select **Sheet Size > B (17in x 11in)**.
11. Click **OK**.

The Drawing environment appears, as shown.

Generating the Base View

The **Base View** tool is activated immediately after starting a new drawing.

1. On the **Drawing View** dialog, select **Orientation > Front**.
2. On the **Drawing View** dialog, set the **Style** to **Visible and Hidden Edges** 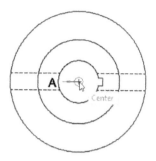.
3. Set **Scale** to **1:1**.
4. Set **Tangent Edges** to **Off**.
5. Place the drawing view on the left side on the drawing sheet, as shown.
6. Click **OK** on the dialog.

Generating the Section View

1. To create the section view, click **Drawing Views > Section View** on the Toolbar.

2. Select the base view.
3. Place the cursor on the center point of the view, as shown.

4. Move the pointer upward and notice the dotted line.

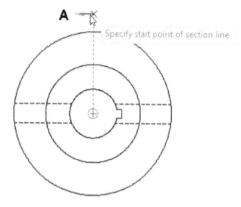

5. Click on the dotted line and move the cursor vertically downwards.
6. Click outside the bottom portion of the view, as shown.

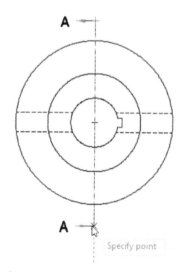

7. Right-click and select **Continue**.

2. Select the base view.
3. On the **Detail View** dialog, set **Style** to **From Parent** .
4. Select **Scale > 2:1**.
5. Specify the center point and boundary point of the detail view, as shown in the figure.

8. Move the cursor toward the right and click to place the section view.

9. Click **OK** on the **Drawing View** dialog.

SECTION A-A
SCALE 1:1

Creating the Detailed View

Now, you have to create a detailed view of the keyway, which is displayed, in the front view.

1. To create a detailed view, click **Drawing Views > Detail View** on the Toolbar.

6. Place the detail view below the base view. Next, click **OK**.

Notice that the label is placed outside the sheet. You need to move it inside.

7. Click on the label, and then select the square point displayed on it.

8. Move the pointer upward and click to place the label, as shown.

DETAIL B
SCALE 2:1

Creating Centermarks and Centerlines

1. To create a center mark, click **Geometry > Center Mark** on the Toolbar.

2. Click on the outer circle of the base view.

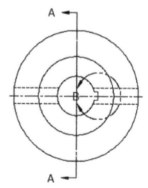

3. To create a centerline, click **Geometry > Centerline** on the Toolbar.

4. Click on the inner horizontal edges of the section view.

Edges selected

2.4

Select geometry or place dimension. Press Shift to toggle snapping

Adding Dimensions

Now, you will add dimensions to the drawing.

1. To add dimensions, click **Dimensions > Dimension** on the Toolbar.

2. Zoom to the section view and select the corner points on the left side, as shown; a dimension is attached to the pointer.

3. Move the pointer toward the left and notice that the dimension is snapped to distance.

4. Click to position the dimension at the snapped point.

5. Likewise, add other linear dimensions to the section view.

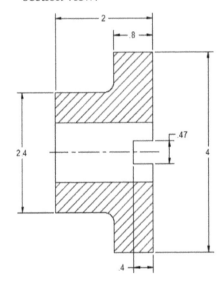

6. Press Esc to deactivate the **Dimension** tool.

7. Double-click on the 2.4-inch linear dimension.

8. Click before the dimension value.

9. Press the **Space** key on your keyboard.
10. On the **Dimension** dialog, select **Insert symbol** drop-down > **Diameter**.
11. Click **Close** on the dialog.

12. Likewise, add the diameter symbol to the linear dimension with the value of 4.

13. On the Toolbar, click **Dimensions > Radius Dimension**.

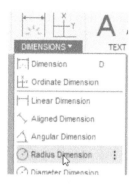

14. Select the fillet on the section view, as shown.
15. Move the pointer diagonally downward, and then click to position the dimension.

16. Right click and select **OK**.

Next, you need to add the diameter dimension.

17. Click **Dimensions > Diameter Dimension** on the Toolbar.

18. Select the center hole on the base view.

19. Place the dimension, as shown in the figure.

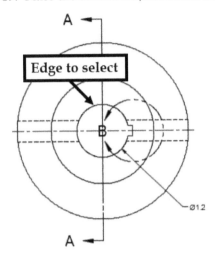

20. Right click and select **OK**.
21. Create the dimensions on the detail view, as shown in the figure.

DETAIL B
SCALE 2:1

22. Expand the **Document Settings** node in the Browser, and place the pointer on the **Display Leading Zeroes** option.
23. Click the **Change Display Leading Zeroes** icon; the **Document Settings** dialog appears.

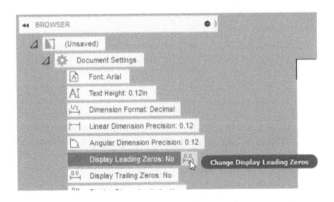

24. On the **Document Settings** dialog, check the **Display** option below the **Angular** box, as shown.
25. Click **OK** on the **Document Settings** dialog.

Zero is added before the dimension values.

Populating the Title Block

1. To populate the title block, double-click on it; the **Properties** dialog appears.
2. Double-click on the TITLE property in the title block.

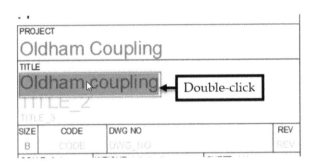

3. Press the SPACEBAR to delete the contents of the property.
4. Type Flange and click on the drawing sheet.

5. Click **Finish Properties** on the **Properties** dialog.

Saving the Drawing

1. Click **Save** on the **Application Bar**.

2. Type-in **Flange** in the **Name** box.
3. Click **Save** to save the file.
4. Click **Close** on the File tab.

TUTORIAL 2

In this tutorial, you will create the drawing of the Oldham coupling assembly created in the previous chapter.

Creating a New Drawing File

1. Open the Oldham coupling file.
2. To start a new drawing, click **File > New Drawing > From Design** on the Application Bar.

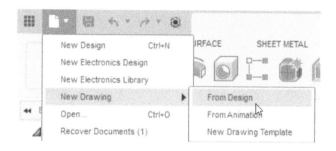

3. On the **Create Drawing** dialog, check the **Full Assembly** option.
4. Select **Template > From Scratch**.
5. Select **Standard > ASME**.
6. Select **Units > in**.
7. Select **Sheet Size > B (17in x 11in)**.
8. Click **OK**.

Generating Base View

The **Base View** tool is activated immediately after starting a new drawing.

1. On the **Drawing View** dialog, select **Orientation > HOME**.
2. On the **Drawing View** dialog, set the **Style** to **Visible Edges** .
3. Set **Scale** to **1:2**.
4. Set **Tangent Edges** to **Full Length** .
5. Place the drawing view on the left side on the drawing sheet, as shown.

6. Click **OK** on the dialog.

Generating the Exploded View

1. To generate the exploded view, click **Drawing Views > Base View** on the Toolbar; the **Drawing View** dialog appears.
2. On the **Drawing View** dialog, select **Representation > Storyboard2**.
3. Select **Orientation > HOME**.
4. Set **Style** to **Visible Edges**.
5. Set **Scale** to **1:2**.
6. Set **Tangent Edges** to **Full Length** .
7. Place the view at the center of the drawing sheet.
8. Click **OK**.

Creating the Parts list

1. To create a parts list, click **Tables > Table** on the Toolbar; the **Table** dialog appears.

2. Select the exploded view from the drawing sheet.
3. Place the part list above the title block.

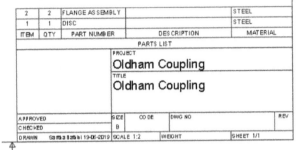

The balloons are added to the view automatically.

Notice that the components of the sub-assembly are not displayed in the parts list. Also, the balloons are not added to the components of the sub-assembly.

Creating the Parts list of the sub-assembly

To create the parts list of the sub-assembly, you need to create a new drawing.

1. Open the Oldham Coupling assembly file.
2. On the Application Bar, click **File > New Drawing > From Design**.
3. Uncheck the **Full Assembly** option on the **Create Drawing** dialog.
4. Select the Flange Assembly from the Browser.

5. On the **Create Drawing** dialog, select **Drawing > Untitled**.
6. Select **Sheet > Create New Sheet**.
7. Click **OK**.
8. On the **Drawing View** dialog, select **Orientation > HOME**.
9. Select **Scale > 1:1**.
10. Select **Tangent Edges > Full Length**.
11. Place the drawing view at the location, as shown.
12. Click **OK**.

13. On the Toolbar, click **Tables > Table**. The view is selected automatically.
14. Place the parts list table above the title block.

15. Double-click on the title block and change the title to Flange Assembly.
16. Click **OK**.
17. Right click on the Sheet2 at the bottom left corner.
18. Select **Rename Sheet**.

19. Type **Flange Assembly** and press Enter.

Saving the Drawing

1. Click **Save** on the **Application Bar**.
2. Type-in **Oldham_Coupling Drawing** in the **Name** box.
3. Click **Save** to save the file.
4. Close the Oldham Coupling assembly and Oldham Coupling Drawing files.

Chapter 5: Sketching

In this chapter, you will learn the sketching tools. You will learn to create:

- Rectangles
- Polygons
- Resolve Sketch
- Constraints
- Splines
- Ellipses
- Circles
- Arcs
- Circular pattern
- Trim Entities
- Fillets and Chamfers

Creating Rectangles

A rectangle is a four-sided object. You can create a rectangle by just specifying its two diagonal corners. However, there are various tools to create a rectangle. You can access these tools from the **Rectangle** menu available on the **Create** panel of the Toolbar. These tools are explained next.

1. On the Toolbar, click the **Solid** tab > **Create** panel > **Create Sketch** and select the XY plane.
2. Click the **Look At** icon on the Sketch Palette.
3. On the **Sketch** contextual tab of the Toolbar, click **Create > Rectangle** menu > **2-Point Rectangle** .
4. Select the origin point to define the first corner.
5. Move the pointer diagonally and click to define

the second corner.

6. On the Toolbar, click the **Create** panel > **Rectangle menu > Center Rectangle**.

7. Click on the graphics window to define the center point.
8. Move the pointer and click to define the corner.

9. On the Toolbar, click the **Sketch** tab > **Create** panel > **Rectangle** menu > **3-Point Rectangle**. This option creates a slanted rectangle.
10. Select two points to define the width and inclination angle of the rectangle.

11. Select the third point to define its height.

Creating Polygons

A Polygon is a shape having many sides ranging from 3 to 1024. In Fusion 360, you can create regular polygons having sides with equal length. You can create a polygon using three methods. These methods are discussed next.

Circumscribed Polygon

The circumscribed polygon has its sides touching an imaginary circle.

1. Start a sketch.
2. On the Toolbar, click the **Sketch** tab > **Create** panel > **Polygon** > **Circumscribed Polygon**.

3. Specify the center point of the polygon.
4. Type **8** in the **Edge Number** box displayed on the polygon.
5. Move the pointer and click to define the size and orientation of the polygon.

Inscribed Polygon

The inscribed polygon has its vertices touching an imaginary circle.

1. On the Toolbar, click the **Sketch** tab > **Create** panel > **Polygon** > **Inscribed Polygon** .
2. Click to define the center of the polygon.
3. Type **6** in the **Edge Number** box.
4. Move the pointer and click to define the size and angle of the polygon.

Edge Polygon

In this method, you will create a polygon by specifying the length of one side and then specifying the number of sides.

1. On the Toolbar, click the **Sketch** tab > **Create** panel > **Polygon** > **Edge Polygon** .
2. Specify the start point of one side.
3. Move the pointer and click to specify the length and angle of the side.

4. Type-in a value in the **Edge number** box.
5. Click to specify the side of the polygon.

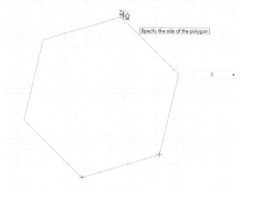

Constraints

Constraints are used to control the shape of a sketch by establishing relationships between the sketch elements. You can add constraints using the tools available in the **Constraints** panel of the **Sketch** contextual tab.

Coincident

This constraint connects a point to another point.

1. On the Toolbar, click **Sketch** tab > **Constraints** panel > **Coincident** .
2. Select two points. The selected points are connected.

Collinear

This constraint two lines collinear to each other.

1. On the Toolbar, click the **Sketch** tab > **Constraints** panel > **Collinear** .
2. Select the two lines, as shown.

Horizontal/Vertical Constraint

This option is used to apply the Horizontal or Vertical constraint. To apply the **Horizontal Constraint**, click on a line that is more inclined to the horizontal axis of the sketch. Next, click the **Horizontal/Vertical** icon on the **Constraints** panel of the **Sketch** contextual tab.

You can also align two points or vertices horizontally. Click the **Horizontal/Vertical** icon on the **Constraints** panel, and then select the two points.

Use the **Horizontal/Vertical** option to apply the vertical constraint to a line that is inclined to the vertical axis. You can also use this option to align two points or vertices vertically.

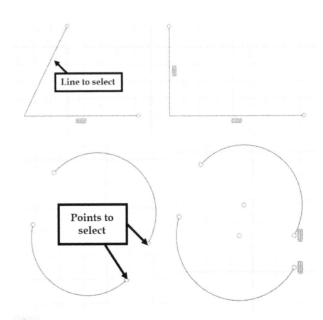

Tangent

This constraint makes an arc, circle, or line tangent to another arc or circle. Click the **Tangent** icon on the **Constraints** panel of the **Sketch** contextual tab. Select a circle, arc, or line. Next, select another circle or arc; the two elements will be tangent to each other.

Parallel

Use the **Parallel** constraint to make two lines parallel to each other. To do this, click the **Parallel** icon in the **Constraints** panel of the **Sketch** contextual tab. Next, select the two lines to be parallel to each other.

Perpendicular

Use the **Perpendicular** constraint to make two entities perpendicular to each other.

Midpoint

Use the **Midpoint** constraint to make a point coincide with the midpoint of a line or arc.

1. Press the Ctrl key and select a line/arc and a point.
2. Click the **Midpoint** icon on the **Constraint** panel of the **Sketch** contextual tab.

Symmetry

Use the **Symmetry** constraint to make two sides of a sketch symmetrical about a line.

1. Create a sketch, as shown.

2. On the Toolbar, click the **Sketch** contextual tab > **Constraints** panel > **Symmetry**.
3. Select the two inclined lines.
4. Select the construction line displayed at the center to define the symmetric line.

The symmetry constraint is applied between the two entities.

Automatic Constraints

Fusion 360 automatically adds constraints when you create sketch elements.

1. Start a new sketch and activate the **Line** tool from the **Create** panel on the **Sketch** contextual tab of the Toolbar.
2. Click the **Look At** icon on the **Sketch Palette**.
3. Click to specify the start point of the line.

4. Move the pointer in the horizontal direction and notice the **Horizontal** constraint flag.
5. Click to create a line with the **Horizontal** constraint.

6. Move the pointer vertically in the upward direction and notice the **Perpendicular** constraint flag.
7. Click to create a line with the **Perpendicular** constraint.

8. Create an inclined line, as shown.

9. Move the pointer along the inclined line and notice the **Parallel** constraint flag.

10. On the Toolbar, click **Sketch** contextual tab > **Create** panel > **Circle** > **Center Diameter Circle**, and then create a circle.
11. Activate the **Line** tool and click on the circle.
12. Move the pointer around the circle and notice that the line maintains the **Tangent** constraint with the circle at a particular position.

13. Click to create a line that is tangent and coincident to the circle. Right click and select **OK**.

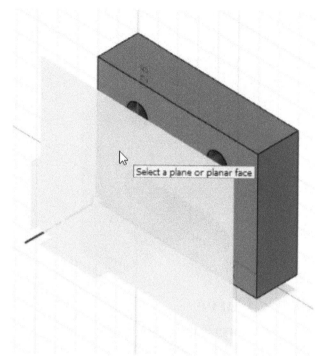

Deleting Constraints

You can delete constraints by using the following method.

- On the Sketch Palette, check the **Show Constraints** option. You can uncheck this option to hide the constraints.
- Select the constraint and press **Delete** on your keyboard.

Project

The **Project** tool helps you to use the edges of the part geometry to create sketch elements.

1. Download the Chapter 5: Sketching folder by reaching us at online.books999@gmail.com.
2. Open the **Project geometry** part file from the folder.
3. Start a sketch on the plane offset to the model face, as shown.

4. On the Toolbar, click the **Sketch** contextual tab > **Create** panel > **Project/Include** > **Project** .
5. Click on the edges of the model, as shown.

6. Click **OK**.
7. Click **Finish Sketch** on the **Sketch Palette**.

The selected edges are projected onto the sketch plane. Also, they are displayed in the magenta color.

Conic Curve

The **Conic Curve** tool is used to create a conic curve. You can use a conic curve to connect two open sketch entities.

1. Create a triangle using the **Polygon** tool.
2. On the Toolbar, click the **Sketch** contextual tab **> Create** panel **> Conic Curve**.
3. Select the start and end limits and control point, as shown.

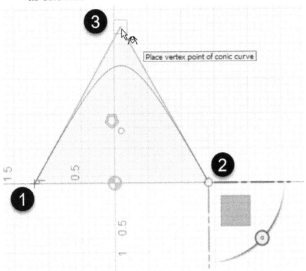

4. Set the **Rho** Value to **0.25**; the preview of the conic curve appears, as shown.

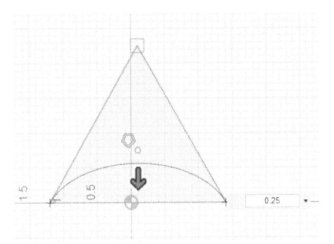

5. Set the **Rho** Value to **0.75** and press Enter.

TUTORIAL 1

In this tutorial, you will create a sketch using the **Line**, **3-Point Arc**, and **Circle** tools.

1. Activate the **Sketch** Environment.
2. On the Toolbar, click **Sketch** contextual tab **> Create** panel **> Line**.
3. Click on the origin point to define the start point of the line.
4. Move the pointer horizontally toward the right and click.

5. Move the pointer upward and click when the perpendicular constraint appears.

6. Right click and select **OK**.
7. On the Toolbar, click the **Sketch** contextual tab > **Create** panel > **Arc** drop-down > **3-Point Arc**.

8. Specify the three points of the arc, as shown.

9. On the Sketch Palette, click **Options** > **Construction** .

10. On the Toolbar, click the **Sketch** contextual tab > **Create** panel > **Line** .
11. Select the origin point of the sketch, move the pointer vertically upwards, and click. Press Esc.

12. On the Toolbar, click the **Sketch** contextual tab > **Create** panel > **Mirror.**

13. Select the arc, horizontal, and vertical lines.
14. On the **Mirror** dialog, click the **Mirror line** button and select the vertical construction line. Click **OK**.

15. On the Sketch Palette, click **Options** > **Construction** .
16. On the Toolbar, click the **Sketch** contextual tab > **Create** panel > **Arc** > **3-Point Arc** .
17. Select the endpoint of the left and right arcs, and then move the pointer upward and click.

23. Add dimensions to the sketch, as shown.

18. Right click and select **OK**.
19. On the Toolbar, click the **Sketch** contextual tab > **Create** panel > **Circle** > **Center Diameter Circle**.
20. Select the centerpoint of the three-point arc, move the pointer outward, and click to create the circle.

21. On the Toolbar, click the **Sketch** contextual tab > **Constraints** panel > **Tangent**.
22. Select two arcs, as shown.

24. On the Toolbar, click the **Sketch** contextual tab > **Constraints** panel > **Coincident**.
25. Select the centerpoint of the arc and the vertical line, as shown.

Selections

26. Add the dimension between the circle and the horizontal line, as shown.

27. Click **Finish Sketch** on the Toolbar.

Ellipses

Ellipses are also non-uniform curves, but they have a regular shape. They are actually splines created in regular closed shapes.

1. Activate the **Sketch** environment.
2. Click **Look At** on the Sketch Palette.

3. On the Toolbar, click the **Sketch** contextual tab > **Create** panel > **Ellipse** ⬭.
4. Pick a point in the graphics window to define the center of the ellipse.
5. Move the pointer and click to define the radius and orientation of the first axis.

6. Move the pointer and click to define the radius of the second axis.

Click and drag the ellipse and notice that it is under-defined. You need to add dimensions and constraints to define the ellipse fully.

7. On the Sketch Palette, click **Options > Construction** ◁.
8. Activate the **Line** tool and select the centerpoint of the ellipse.
9. Move the pointer horizontally toward the right and click. Press **Esc**.

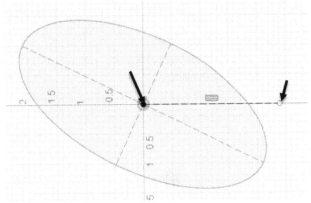

10. On the Toolbar, click the **Sketch** contextual tab

    > Create panel **> Sketch Dimension** .
11. Select the horizontal line and the major axis of the ellipse.
12. Move the pointer between the selected lines and click to position the angled dimension.

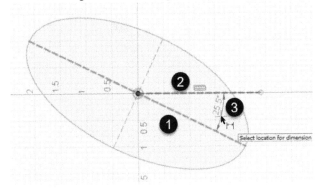

13. Type 15 and press Enter.
14. Select the major axis.
15. Move the pointer downward and click to position the dimension.
16. Type 1.96 and press Enter.
17. Likewise, add the dimension to the minor axis; the sketch is fully defined.

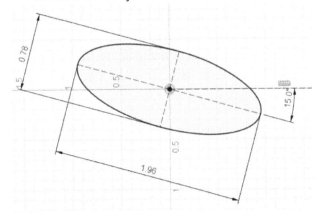

Concentric Constraint

Use the **Concentric** Constraint to make two center points of circles, arcs, or ellipses coincident with each other.

1. Create two circles, as shown.

2. On the Toolbar, click the **Sketch** contextual tab **>**

    Constraints panel **> Concentric** .
3. Select the two circles to make them concentric.

4. Press Esc.
5. On the Toolbar, click the **Sketch** contextual tab **>**

    Create panel **> Sketch Dimension** .
6. Select the inner circle, move the point upward, and click to position the dimension.
7. Type **1.96** and press Enter.

72

8. Likewise, add dimension to the remaining circle and change its value to **5.5**.
9. Press Esc.

Center Point Arc

The Center Point Arc tool creates an arc by using three points (center, start, and endpoints).

1. On the Toolbar, click the **Sketch** contextual tab >

   Create panel > Arc > Center Point Arc .
2. Select the point on the circle, as shown below.

3. Move the pointer down and click on the circle.

4. Move the pointer leftwards and up, and then click on the circle.

5. Right click and select **OK**.
6. On the Toolbar, click the **Sketch** contextual tab >

   Create panel > **Sketch Dimension** .
7. Select the arc, move the pointer, and then click to position the dimension.
8. Type **0.98**, and then press Enter.

9. On the Toolbar, click the **Sketch** contextual tab > **Create** panel > **Constraints** >

   Horizontal/Vertical .

10. Click on the center point of the circle and arc.

Circular Pattern

The **Circular Pattern** tool creates an arrangement of objects around a point in circular form.

1. On the Toolbar, click the **Sketch** contextual tab > **Create** panel > **Circular Pattern** .

2. Select the arc.

3. Click the **Select** button next to the **Center Point** option.

4. Select the center of the circle; the preview of the circular pattern appears.

5. Type **4** in the **Quantity** box.

6. Select **Type > Full**.

7. Click **OK**.

Trim

The **Trim** tool removes the unwanted entities of a sketch using a trimming element.

1. On the Toolbar, click the **Sketch** contextual tab > **Modify** panel > **Trim** .

2. Click on the portions of the sketch, as shown.

3. Right click and select **OK**.

4. Click **Finish Sketch**.

Extend

The **Extend** tool is similar to the **Trim** tool, but its use is the opposite of it. This tool is used to extend lines, arcs, and other open entities to connect to other objects.

1. Create a sketch, as shown below.

2. Click the **Sketch** contextual tab > **Modify** panel > **Extend** ⟶⎮ on the Toolbar.
3. Select the horizontal open line. This will extend the line up to the arc.

Likewise, extend the other elements, as shown.

4. Trim the unwanted portions.

Offset

The **Offset** tool creates parallel copies of lines, circles, and arcs.

1. On the Toolbar, click the **Sketch** contextual tab > **Modify** panel > **Offset** .

2. Select an entity and notice that all the connected entities are selected.

3. Type-in the offset distance in the value box attached to the offset copy.

4. Click **Flip** icon to define the offset side.

5. Click **OK**.

Text

Texts are used to provide information on the models such as company name, model specifications, and so on.

1. Start a new sketch.

2. On the Toolbar, click the **Sketch** contextual tab > **Create** panel > **Text** .

3. Specify a point in the graphics window.

4. Click on the **Text** box in the **Text** dialog, and then type FUSION 360.

5. On the **Text** dialog, set **Text Style** to **Bold**.

6. Select **Font > Arial**.

7. On the dialog, use the **Horizontal Flip** or **Vertical Flip** icons to flip the text.

8. Type 0.45 in the **Height** box.

9. Click and drag the angle handle displayed in the graphics window (or) type-in a value in the **Angle** box.

10. Click **OK**.

Chapter 6: Additional Modeling Tools

In this chapter, you create models using additional modeling tools. You will learn to:

- Create slots
- Create circular patterns
- Create holes
- Create chamfers
- Create shells
- Create rib features
- Create coils
- Create a loft feature
- Create a thread
- Create a sweep feature
- Replace faces
- Create a variable fillet

TUTORIAL 1

In this tutorial, you create the model shown in the figure:

Creating the First Feature

1. Create a new project with the name **Autodesk Fusion 360 Basics Tutorial** (See Chapter 2, Tutorial 1, Creating a New Project section to learn how to create a new project).
2. Click the **Create sketch** button on the **Create** panel of the Toolbar and select the XZ Plane.
3. Click the **Look At** icon on the Sketch Palette.
4. Click the **Sketch** tab > **Create** panel > **Circle** drop-down > **Center Diameter Circle** on the Toolbar.
5. Draw a circle by selecting the origin point as its center (See Chapter 2, Tutorial 1, Starting a Sketch section to learn how to create a new circle).
6. Click the **Line** button.
7. Specify a point at the top left outside the circle.
8. Move the pointer horizontally and notice the Horizontal constraint symbol.
9. Click outside the circle — Press Esc to deactivate the **Line** tool.

10. On the Toolbar, click the **Sketch** tab > **Modify** panel > **Trim** .
11. Click on the portions of the sketch to trim, as shown below.

12. Activate the **Sketch Dimension** tool and select the horizontal line.
13. Right click and select **Pick Circle/Arc Tangent**.
14. Select the bottom quadrant point of the arc.
15. Move the pointer toward the left and click to place the dimension.
16. Type 1.102 and press Enter.
17. Select the arc and place the dimension.
18. Type 0.63 and press Enter.

20. Select the origin as the center point.
21. Move the cursor outward and click in the first quadrant of the circle to specify the start point of the slot arc.
22. Move the cursor and click on the fourth quadrant of the circle to specify the endpoint of the slot arc.

19. Click the **Sketch** tab > **Create** panel > **Slot** dropdown > **Center Point Arc Slot** on the Toolbar.

23. Move the cursor outward from the arc and click.

78

24. Click the **Sketch** tab > **Create** panel > **Sketch Dimension** button on Toolbar.
25. Select the start point of the slot arc.
26. Select the center point of the slot arc.
27. Select the endpoint of the slot arc.

28. Move the pointer outward and place the angular dimension of the slot.
29. Enter **30** in the box and press Enter.

30. Click the **Construction** button on the **Sketch Palette**.
31. Click the **Line** button on the **Create** panel.
32. Draw a horizontal line passing through the origin.

33. Click the **Symmetry** button on the **Constraints** panel.
34. Select the end caps of the slot.
35. Select the construction line; the slot is made symmetric about the construction line.

36. Apply the other dimensions to the slot.

43. Select **Type > Angle**.
44. Type **180** in the **Total Angle** box.

The preview of the circular pattern appears.

45. Click **OK** to create the circular pattern.

37. On the Toolbar, click the **Sketch** tab **> Create panel > Circular Pattern**; the **Circular Pattern** dialog appears.
38. On the Toolbar, click the **Sketch** tab **> Select panel > Window Selection**.

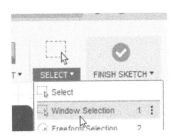

39. Select all the elements of the slot by creating a selection window (press and hold the left mouse button and drag the pointer from left to right).

46. Click the **Finish Sketch** button on the Toolbar.
47. Extrude the sketch up to 0.236 distance (See Chapter 2, Tutorial 1, Creating the Base Feature section to learn how to create an extruded feature).

40. Click the **Select** button located on the right side of the **Center Point** option.
41. Select the origin point of the sketch.
42. Enter **4** in the **Quantity** box.

Creating a Counterbore Hole

In this section, you will create a counterbore hole concentric to the circular face.

1. On the Toolbar, click the **Solid** tab > **Create** panel > **Hole** ; the **Hole** dialog appears.

2. Set the parameters in the **Hole** dialog, as shown in the figure.

Adding the Second feature

1. Create a sketch on the back face of the model (use the **Orbit** tool available on the Navigation bar to rotate the model).

2. Extrude the sketch up to 0.078 distance.

3. Click on the front face of the model; the preview of the hole appears.

Now, you need to specify the reference.

4. Select the circular edge of the front face; the hole is made concentric to the edge.

5. Specify the size values on the **Hole** dialog, as shown.

6. Click **OK**; the counterbore hole is created.

Creating a Threaded hole

In this section, you will create a hole using a sketch point.

1. Click the **Create Sketch** button on the **Create** panel and select the front face of the model.
2. Click **Look At** on the Sketch Palette.
3. On the Toolbar, click the **Sketch** tab > **Create** panel > **Point**.

4. Place the point on the front face of the model.
5. Click the **Horizontal /Vertical** button on the **Constraint** panel.
6. Select the point and sketch origin; the point becomes horizontal to the origin.

7. Create a horizontal dimension of 0.354 between the point and origin.

8. Click **Finish Sketch**.
9. On the Toolbar, click the **Solid** tab > **Create** panel > **Hole**; the **Hole** dialog appears.
10. Select the sketch point.
11. Select **Extents > All**.

12. Select the **Counterbore** option.

13. Select the **Tapped** option.

14. Set **Thread Offset** to **Full** .

15. Set the **Thread Type** to **ANSI Unified Screw Threads**.

16. Set the **Size** to **0.073**.

17. Set the **Designation** to **1-64 UNC**.

18. Select **Class > 2B**.

19. Set the **Direction** to **Right Hand**.

20. Set the **Counterbore Diameter** to 0.118.

21. Set the **Counterbore Depth** to 0.039.

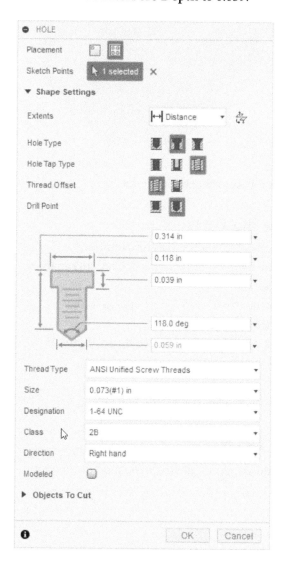

Creating a Circular Pattern

1. On the Toolbar, click **Solid** tab **> Create** panel **> Pattern** drop-down **> Circular Pattern**; the **Circular Pattern** dialog appears.

2. Select **Pattern Type > Features**.

3. Select the threaded hole created in the previous section.

4. Click the **Select** button next to the **Axis** option.

5. Select the outer cylindrical face of the model.

6. Select **Type > Full**.

7. Enter **6** in the **Quantity** box.

8. Click **OK** to create the circular pattern.

22. Click **OK** to create the hole.

Creating Chamfers

1. On the **Solid** tab of the Toolbar, click **Modify > Chamfer**.

2. Select **Chamfer Type > Distance and angle** on the dialog.
3. Select the circular edge of the counterbore hole.

4. Enter 0.022 in the **Distance** box and 60 in the **Angle** box.

5. Click **OK** to create the chamfer.

Saving the Part

1. Click **Save** 💾 on the **Application bar**.
2. On the **Save** window, type-in **Ch6_tut1** in the **Name** box.
3. Click the down arrow button next to the **Location** box.
4. Select **Autodesk Fusion 360 Basics Tutorial** from the **Project** list.
5. Click **Save** to save the file.
6. Click the **Close** icon on the File tab.

TUTORIAL 2

In this tutorial, you will create the model shown in the figure.

Creating the first feature

1. On the Toolbar, click the **Sketch** tab > **Create** panel > **Create Sketch** .

2. Select the YZ plane.

3. Click the **Look At** icon on the Sketch Palette.

4. Draw an L-shaped sketch using the **Line** tool and dimension it.

5. On the Toolbar, click the **Sketch** tab > **Modify** panel > **Offset** .

6. Select the sketch, and then drag the offset handle in the upward direction.

7. Type 0.472 in the **Offset position** box.

8. Click **OK**.

9. Click the **Line** button and draw lines closing the offset sketch.

10. Click **Finish Sketch**.

11. Click the **Solid** tab > **Create** panel > **Extrude** on the Toolbar.

12. Click on the region enclosed by the sketch.

13. Select **Direction** > **Symmetric** option from the **Extrude** dialog.

14. Set **Measurement** to **Whole Length** .

15. Set the **Distance** to 1.575.
16. Click **OK** to create the first feature.
17. Click the **Home** icon next to the ViewCube.

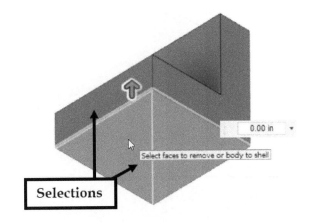

Creating the Shell feature

You can create a shell feature by removing the face of the model and applying thickness to other faces.

1. Click the **Solid** tab > **Modify** panel > **Shell** on the Toolbar; the **Shell** dialog appears.

Now, you need to select the faces to remove.

2. Select the top face and the back face of the model.

3. Select the front face and the bottom face of the model.

4. Set **Thickness** to 0.197.
5. Click **OK** to shell the model.

Creating the Third feature

1. Click the **Solid** tab> **Create** panel > **Create Sketch** on the Toolbar.

2. Select the front face of the model.
3. Click the **Look At** icon on the Sketch Palette.
4. Click the **Sketch** tab > **Create** panel > **Slot** drop-down > **Center to Center Slot** on the Toolbar.

5. Draw a slot by selecting the first, second, and third points, as shown.

6. On the Toolbar, click the **Sketch** tab > **Constraints** panel > **Midpoint** △.
7. Select the lower center point of the slot.
8. Select the lower horizontal edge of the model, as shown.

9. Apply dimensions to the slot.

10. Click **Finish Sketch**.
11. Click the **Solid** tab > **Create** panel > **Extrude** on the Toolbar.
12. Click on the three regions of the sketch.

13. Select the **To Object** option from the **Extent** drop-down.
14. Press and hold the left mouse button on the top face, and then select the back face from the dialog.

15. Select **Chain Faces > Extend Faces** .
16. Select **Operation > Join** from the dialog.
17. Click **OK** to create the feature.

Creating a Cut Feature

1. Start a sketch on the front face of the model.
2. Click the **Look At** icon on the Sketch Palette.
3. Click the **Sketch** tab > **Create** panel > **Slot** drop-down > **Center to Center Slot** on the Toolbar.

4. Create a vertical slot.
5. On the Toolbar, click the **Sketch** tab > **Constraints** panel > **Concentric**.
6. Select a slot end cap.
7. Select a circular edge of the model; the slot end cap is made concentric with the circular edge.
8. Likewise, make the other end cap of the slot concentric to the circular edge.
9. Add a dimension to the sketch, as shown.

R0.118

10. Finish the sketch.
11. Click the **Solid** tab > **Create** panel > **Extrude** on the Toolbar.
12. Click on the region enclosed by the sketch.
13. Select the **All** option from the **Extent** drop-down.
14. Select **Operation > Cut**.
15. Click the **Flip** icon, if the arrow on the sketch points in the forward direction.
16. Click **OK** to create the cut feature.

Creating the Rib Feature

In this section, you will create a rib feature at the center of the model.

1. Click the **Solid** tab > **Create** panel > **Create Sketch** on the Toolbar.
2. Expand the **Origin** folder, and then select the YZ Plane from the Browser.

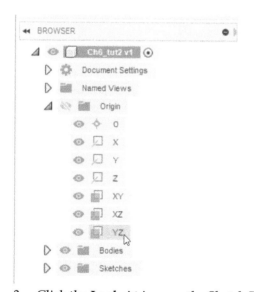

3. Click the **Look At** icon on the Sketch Palette.
4. Click the **Sketch** tab > **Create** panel > **Line** on the Toolbar.
5. Draw the sketch, as shown below.

6. On the Toolbar, click **Sketch** tab > **Constraints** > **Coincident**.
7. Select the endpoint of the inclined line and the vertex point of the top edge.

8. Select the endpoint of the vertical line and the vertical edge, as shown.

9. Select the endpoint of the vertical line and the vertical edge.

10. Add dimension to the sketch.

11. Click **Finish Sketch** on the Toolbar.
12. Click **Solid** tab > **Create** panel > **Rib** on the Toolbar; the **Rib** dialog appears.

13. Select the sketch.
14. Set **Thickness** to 0.197.
15. Select **Depth Options** > **To Next**.
16. Select **Thickness Options** > **Symmetric**.
17. Click **OK** to create the rib feature.

18. Save the model and close it.

TUTORIAL 3

In this tutorial, you will create a helical spring using the **Coil** tool.

Creating the Coil

1. Click the **Solid** tab > **Create** panel > **Coil** on the Toolbar and select the XY Plane.
2. Select the origin point to define the center of the coil.
3. Move the cursor outward and click to create a circle.

4. On the **Coil** dialog, type **1.575** in the **Diameter** box.
5. Select **Type > Revolution and Pitch**.
6. Type **8** in the **Revolutions** box.
7. Type **0.59** in the **Pitch** box.
8. Select **Section > Circular**.
9. Select **Section Position > On Center**.
10. Type **0.236** in the **Section Size** box.

Click and drag the Angle handle and notice that the coil is tapered.

11. Type **0** in the **Angle** box.
12. Click **OK** to create the coil.
13. Save and close the file.

TUTORIAL 4

In this tutorial, you create a shampoo bottle using the **Loft**, **Extrude**, **Press Pull**, and **Sweep** tools.

Creating the First Section and Rails

To create a swept feature, you need to create sections and guide curves.

1. Click the **Solid** tab > **Create** panel > **Create Sketch** on the Toolbar.
2. Select the XY plane.
3. Click the **Look At** icon on the Sketch Palette.
4. Click the **Sketch** tab > **Create** panel > **Ellipse** on the Toolbar.
5. Draw the ellipse by selecting the points, as shown.

6. On the Toolbar, click the **Sketch** tab > **Create** panel > **Sketch Dimension**.
7. Select the ellipse, move the cursor downward, and click.
8. Type 1.968 and press Enter.
9. Select the ellipse, move the cursor toward left, and click.
10. Type 0.984 and press Enter.

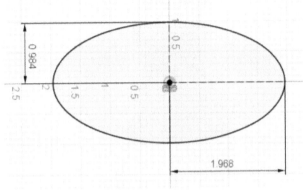

11. Click **Finish Sketch**.
12. Click the **Home** icon on the top left corner of the **ViewCube**.
13. Click the **Solid** tab > **Create** panel > **Create Sketch** on the Toolbar.
14. Click the **Look At** icon on the Sketch Palette.
15. Select the XZ plane from the graphics window.
16. Click the **Sketch** tab > **Create** panel > **Spline** drop-down > **Fit Point Spline** on the Toolbar.
17. Select a point on the horizontal axis of the sketch; a rubber band curve is attached to the cursor

18. Move the cursor up and specify the second point of the spline; a curve is attached to the cursor.

19. Move the cursor up and specify the third point.

20. Likewise, specify the other points of the spline, as shown.
21. Click the right mouse button and select **OK**. The spline will be similar to the one shown in the figure.

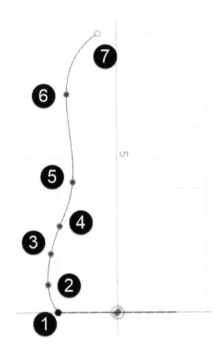

22. Right click and select **Sketch > Line** from the Marking Menu.
23. On the Sketch Palette, click **Options >**

Construction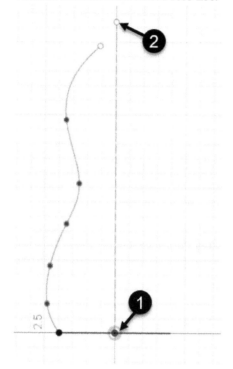

24. Select the origin point of the sketch, move the pointer vertically upward and click to create a vertical construction line. Press Esc.

25. Make the first point of the spline coincident with the ellipse, if not already coincident.

26. On the Toolbar, click the **Sketch** tab > **Create** panel > **Sketch Dimension**.
27. Select the second point of the spline and the construction line.
28. Move the cursor and click to place the dimension.
29. Type 2.362 in the box and press Enter.

30. Apply the other horizontal dimensions to the spline, as shown in the figure.

31. Select the origin point of the sketch and the top endpoint of the spline.
32. Move the pointer toward the right and click.
33. Type 8.858 in the box and press Enter.

34. Likewise, create other dimensions, as shown.

35. Click the **Sketch** tab > **Create** panel > **Mirror** on the Toolbar; the **Mirror** dialog appears.

36. Select the spline. Make sure that you select the curve and not the points.

37. Click the **Select** button next to the **Mirror line** option on the **Mirror** dialog, and then select the construction line.

38. Click **OK**.

39. Click **Finish Sketch** on the Toolbar.

Creating the second section

1. Click the **Home** icon on the top left corner of the ViewCube.

2. Click the **Solid** tab > **Construct** panel > **Offset Plane** on the Toolbar.

3. Select the XY plane from the Browser.

4. Enter **8.858** in the **Distance** box.

5. Click **OK**.

6. On the Toolbar, click the **Solid** tab > **Create** panel > **Create Sketch**.

7. Select the newly created datum plane.

8. Click the **Look At** icon on the Sketch Palette.

9. On the Toolbar, click the **Sketch** tab > **Create** panel > **Circle** drop-down > **2-Point Circle**.

10. Select the endpoints of the two splines, as shown.

Points to select

11. Right click and select **OK**.

12. Click and drag the circle downward and notice that it is under-defined.

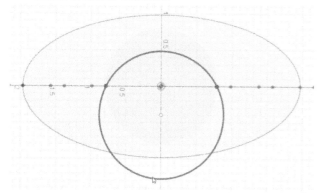

13. On the Toolbar, click the **Sketch** tab >

Constraints panel > **Coincident** .

14. Select the centerpoint of the circle and the origin point of the sketch; the circle is fully-defined.

15. Click **Finish Sketch** on the Toolbar.

Creating the Loft feature

1. Click the **Home** icon on the top left corner of the **ViewCube**.

2. To create a loft feature, click the **Solid** tab > **Create** panel > **Loft** on the Toolbar; the **Loft** dialog appears.

3. Click on the region enclosed by the ellipse.

4. Click the plus + icon in the **Profiles** section.

5. Click on the region enclosed by the circle.

6. Select **Guide Type > Rails** option from the dialog.

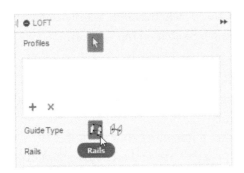

7. Select the cursor icon next to the **Rails** option.
8. Select the first spline.
9. Click the plus ✛ icon in the **Rails** section.
10. Select the second spline.

11. Click **OK** to create the loft feature.

Creating the Extruded feature

1. On the Toolbar, click **Create** panel > **Create Sketch**.
2. Select the top face of the sweep feature.

3. On the Toolbar, click the **Sketch** tab > **Create** panel > **Circle** > **Center Diameter Circle**.
4. Select the origin point, move the cursor outside, and click to create a circle.
5. Right click and select **OK**.
6. Right click and select **Sketch > Sketch Dimension**.
7. Select the circle, move the cursor outward, and click.
8. Type 1.574 and press Enter.

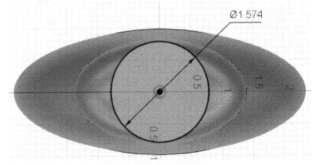

9. Click **Finish Sketch** on the Toolbar.
10. Click the **Extrude** button on the **Create** panel.

11. Extrude the circle up to 1 in.

Creating an Emboss

1. Click the **Solid** tab > **Construct** panel > **Offset Plane** on the Toolbar.
2. Select the XZ plane from the Browser.
3. Enter **2** in the **Distance** box and click **OK**.

4. Click the **Solid** tab > **Create** panel > **Create Sketch** on the Toolbar.
5. Click the **Look At** icon on the Sketch Palette.
6. Select the newly created datum plane
7. Click the **Sketch** tab > **Create** panel > **Ellipse** on the Toolbar.
8. Draw the ellipse by selecting the points, as shown.

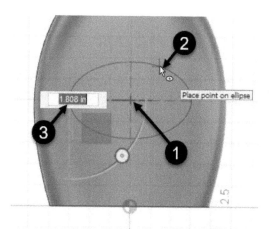

On the Toolbar, click the **Sketch** tab > **Create** panel > **Sketch Dimension**.

9. Select the ellipse, move the cursor downward, and click.
10. Type 2 and press Enter.
11. Select the ellipse, move the cursor toward left, and click.
12. Type 1.35 and press Enter.
13. Select the origin point of the sketch and the center point of the ellipse.
14. Move the cursor toward left and click to place the dimension between the selected point.
15. Type 2.55 and press Enter.
16. On the Toolbar, click **Constraints** panel > **Horizontal/Vertical**.
17. Select the center point of the ellipse and the sketch origin; the sketch is fully-constrained.
18. Click **Finish Sketch**.

19. Click the **Home** icon on the top left corner of the **ViewCube**.
20. Click the **Solid** tab > **Modify** panel > **Press Pull**

on the Toolbar; the **Press Pull** dialog appears.

21. Click on the region enclosed by the sketch.
22. Select **Extent > To Object**.
23. Click on the surface of the loft feature.
24. Set **Solution** to **Min Solution** ⊥.
25. Select **Chain Faces > Chain Faces** ⊀.
26. Set the **Offset** to -0.125.
27. Select **Operation > New Body**.
28. Click **OK** to create a new body.

29. On the Toolbar, click **Modify > Combine** .
30. Select the Target and Tool bodies, as shown.

31. Select **Operation > Cut**.
32. Click **OK**.

Creating Fillets

1. Click **Modify > Fillet** on the Toolbar of the **Solid** tab; the **Fillet** dialog appears.

2. Click on the bottom and top edges of the loft feature.

3. Select **Type > Constant Radius**.
4. Set **Radius** to 0.2.
5. Click **OK**.
6. Right click and select **Repeat Fillet**.

7. Select the edges of the emboss.

8. Set **Radius** to 0.04.
9. Click **OK**.

3. Set **Inside Thickness** to 0.03.
4. Click **OK** to create the shell.

Shelling the Model

1. Click **Modify > Shell** on the Toolbar of the **Solid** tab; the **Shell** dialog appears.

2. Select the top face of the cylindrical feature.

Adding Threads

1. On the Toolbar, click **Solid** tab > **Construct** panel > **Offset Plane**.
2. Click on the top face of the model geometry.
3. Set the **Distance** value to -0.196.
4. Click **OK**; a new plane is created.

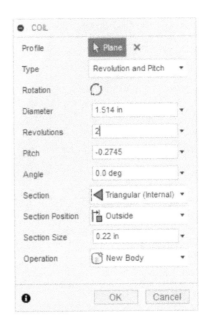

5. On the Toolbar, click **Solid** tab > **Create** panel > **Coil**.
6. Select the newly created plane.
7. Select the origin point of the sketch.
8. Click on the Top face of the ViewCube; the orientation is changed to top.
9. Select a point on the inner edge of the shell feature, as shown.

10. Click the **Home** icon located at the top left corner of the ViewCube; the view orientation is changed to Home.
11. Specify the settings on the **Coil** dialog, as shown.

12. Click **OK**.
13. On the Toolbar, click **Solid** tab > **Create** panel > **Create Sketch**.
14. Select the YZ Plane.
15. On the Toolbar, click the **Sketch** tab > **Create** panel > **Project/Include** drop-down > **Include 3D Geometry**.
16. Click on the inner edge of the coil feature, as shown.

17. In the **Browser**, expand the **Bodies** folder and turn off the visibility icon next to the Body3.

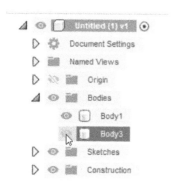

18. Click **Finish Sketch** on the Toolbar.
19. Click the **Solid** tab > **Create** panel > **Create Sketch** on the Toolbar.
20. Select the XZ Plane.
21. On the Navigation Bar, click **Display Settings > Visual Style > Wireframe**.

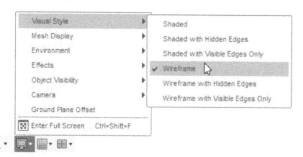

22. Click the **Look At** icon on the Sketch Palette.
23. On the Toolbar, click the **Sketch** tab > **Create** panel > **Line**.
24. Click **Construction** on the **Sketch Palette**.
25. Zoom to the top portion of the model.
26. Create a horizontal construction line passing through the endpoint of the helical curve, as shown.

27. Deactivate the **Construction** icon on the **Sketch Palette**.
28. On the Toolbar, click the **Sketch** tab > **Create** panel > **Line**.
29. Create a closed profile, as shown.

30. On the Toolbar, click the **Sketch** tab > **Modify** panel > **Fillet** .
31. Select the two corners of the sketch, as shown.

32. Type 0.04 in the **Fillet radius** box and press Enter.
33. Activate the **Sketch Dimension** tool and apply dimensions to the sketch, as shown.

panel > **Sweep**.

40. On the **Sweep** dialog, select **Type > Path + Guide Surface**.
41. Click on the region enclosed by the sketch.
42. Click the **Select** button next to the **Path** option.
43. Select the helical curve.
44. Click the **Select** button next to the **Guide Surface** option.
45. Select the inner face of the shell feature, as shown.

34. On the Toolbar, click the **Sketch** tab > **Constraints** panel > **Coincident**.
35. Select the vertical line of the sketch and the endpoint of the helical curve, as shown.

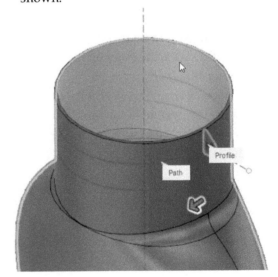

36. Click **Finish Sketch**.
37. Click the **Home** icon located at the top left corner of the ViewCube; the view orientation is changed to Home.
38. On the Navigation Bar, click **Display Settings > Visual Style > Shaded with Visible Edges Only.**
39. On the Toolbar, click the **Solid** tab > **Create**

46. Select **Operation > Join**.
47. Click **OK** to create the sweep feature.

102

48. In the Browser, right click on the XZ Plane, and then select **Create Sketch**.

49. On the Toolbar, click the **Sketch** tab **> Create panel > Project/Include > Project** .
50. Select the edges of the end face of the sweep feature.

51. Click **OK**.
52. Draw a straight line connecting the endpoints of the projected elements.

53. Click **Finish Sketch**.
54. Activate the **Revolve** tool and click on the region enclosed by the sketch.
55. Click the **Select** button next to the **Axis** option.
56. Select the vertical line of the sketch.
57. On the dialog, select **Type > Angle**, and then type-in **-100** in the **Angle** box.
58. Select **Direction > One side**.
59. Select **Operation > Join**.

60. Click **OK**.
61. Likewise, blend the other end of the thread. Note that you need to enter a negative angle value.

62. Save the model and close it.

TUTORIAL 5

In this tutorial, you create a chair, as shown.

Creating a 3D Sketch

1. On the Toolbar, click the **Solid** tab > **Create panel** > **Create Sketch**.
2. Select the XY Plane.
3. On the **Sketch Palette**, check the **3D Sketch** option.
4. On the Toolbar, click the **Sketch** tab > **Create panel** > **Line**.
5. Select the origin point of the sketch.
6. Move the pointer along the X-axis (red line).
7. Type 12 and press Enter.

8. On the Toolbar, click the **Sketch** tab > **Create panel** > **Line**.
9. Select the endpoint of the previous line.
10. Move the pointer towards front.
11. Type 20 and press Enter.

12. On the Toolbar, click the **Sketch** tab > **Create panel** > **Line**.
13. Select the endpoint of the previous line.
14. Move the pointer in the vertical direction; the 3D gizmo appears.

15. Move the pointer along the Z-axis of the 3D gizmo.
16. Type 18 and press Enter.

21. Activate the **Line** tool.
22. Select the endpoint of the previous line.
23. Move the pointer along the Z-axis.
24. Type 18 and press Enter.

17. On the Toolbar, click the **Sketch** tab > **Create** panel > **Line**.
18. Select the endpoint of the vertical line.
19. Move the pointer along the Y-axis.
20. Type 22 and press Enter.

25. Activate the **Line** tool.
26. Select the endpoint of the previous line.
27. Move the pointer along the X-axis.
28. Type 24 and press Enter.

29. Likewise, create the other lines, as shown.

30. Right click and select **OK**.
31. On the Toolbar, click the **Sketch** tab > **Modify**

    panel > **Fillet**   .
32. Select the corner point of the sketch, as shown.

33. Type-in 3 in the **Fillet radius** box and press Enter on your keyboard.
34. Likewise, fillet the other corners, a shown.

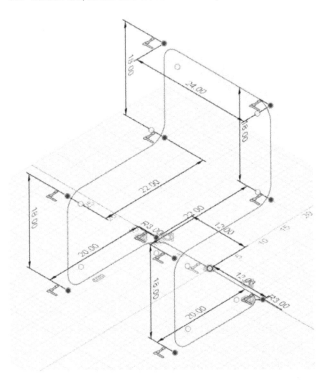

Creating the Pipe feature

1. On the Toolbar, click the **Solid** tab > **Create**

   panel > **Pipe**   .
2. Click on the sketch.
3. On the **Pipe** dialog, select **Section > Circular**.
4. Type-in 1.25 in the **Section Size** box.
5. Check the **Hollow** option.
6. Type-in 0.25 in the **Section Thickness** box.
7. Click **OK** to create the pipe feature.

8. On the Toolbar, click the **Solid** tab **> Create panel > Create Sketch**.
9. Click on the YZ Plane.

10. Check the **Slice** option on the Sketch Palette.

11. Click the **Look At** icon on the Sketch Palette.
12. Draw the circles and dimension them, as shown.

13. Click **Finish Sketch**.
14. Activate the **Extrude** tool and click on the outer loop of the sketch.

15. On the **Extrude** dialog, select **Direction > Two Sides**.
16. In the **Side 1** section, select **Extent > To Object**.
17. Select the right side of the pipe, as shown.
18. In the **Side 2** section, select **Extent > To Object**.
19. Select the left side of the pipe,

23. Extrude the remaining loops, as shown.

20. Select **Operation > Join**.
21. Click **OK** to extrude the sketch.

24. Hide the sketch.

22. On the Browser, turn on the visibility icon next to Sketch 2; the sketch is displayed.

Creating the Freeform feature

1. On the Toolbar, click the **Solid** tab **> Construct** panel **> Tangent Plane**.

2. Select the round face, as shown.

3. In the **Browser**, expand the **Origin** folder, and then click the XY Plane.
4. Click **OK** to create a plane tangent to the selected round face and parallel to the XY plane.

5. Start a sketch on the new plane.

6. Click the **Look At** icon on the Sketch Palette.
7. On the Toolbar, click the **Sketch** tab >**Create panel > Point**.
8. Place a point on the sketch plane and add dimension and constraint to position it.

9. Click **Finish Sketch**.
10. Click the **Home** icon on the top-left corner of the ViewCube.
11. On the Toolbar, click the **Solid** tab > **Construct > Tangent Plane**.
12. Click on the top horizontal portion of the sweep feature to create a plane tangent to it.
13. In the Browser, click the XZ Plane.

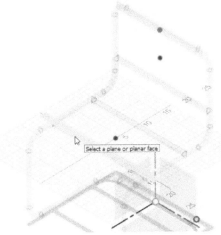

and then turn on the two tangent planes.

23. On the Toolbar, click **Create > Box**.
24. Select the plane tangent to the extruded feature.

14. Type **180** in the **Angle** box.
15. Click **OK**.
16. Start a sketch on the new plane.
17. Click the **Look At** icon on the Sketch Palette.
18. Place a point and add dimension and constraint to it.

25. On the **Box** dialog, click **Rectangle Type > Center**.
26. Select the sketch point to define the location of the freeform box.
27. Move the pointer outward and click.
28. On the **Box** dialog, type 28 in the **Length** box.
29. Type 19 on the **Width** box.
30. Type 4 in the **Height** box.
31. Type 4, 1, and 2 in the **Length Faces**, **Width Faces**, and **Height Faces** boxes, respectively.
32. Select **Symmetry > Mirror**.
33. Check the **Length Symmetry** option.
34. Click **OK** to create the freeform shape.

19. Click **Finish Sketch**.
20. Click the **Home** icon next to the ViewCube.
21. On the Toolbar, click the **Solid** tab > **Create** panel > **Create Form**.
22. In the Browser, expand the **Construction** folder,

The symmetry line is displayed at the center.

Editing the Freeform Shape

1. On the Toolbar, click the **Form** tab > **Modify**
   panel > **Edit Form** .
2. Click on the top face of the freeform shape.

3. Click on the arrow pointing upwards.
4. Drag it downwards 2 inches, as shown in the figure below.

5. Click **OK** on the dialog.
6. On the Toolbar, click the **Form** tab > **Modify**
   panel > **Edit Form** .
7. Click on the edge at the front.

8. Drag the vertical arrow downwards.

9. Click **OK** on the **Edit Form** dialog.
10. Activate the Freeform **Box** tool.
11. Select the tangent plane and click on the sketch point.

Select a plane or planar face

Specify center point

12. Move the pointer in the diagonal direction and click.

13. On the **Box** dialog, type-in 27, 16, and -3 in the **Length**, **Width**, and **Height** boxes, respectively.

14. Type **2** in the **Length Faces**, **Width Faces**, and **Height Faces** boxes, respectively

15. Click **OK**, and then click **Finish Form** on the Toolbar.

16. Save and close the file.

TUTORIAL 6

In this tutorial, you create a bolt.

Creating the Base Feature

1. On the Toolbar, click the **Solid** tab > **Create** panel > **Cylinder** .

2. Click on the YZ Plane.

112

3. Click the origin point of the sketch to define the center point of the circle.

4. Move the pointer and type-in 0.75 in the box, and then press Enter.

5. Type-in 3 in the **Height** box and press Enter.

Creating the second feature

1. Start a sketch on the YZ Plane.

2. Click the **Look At** icon on the Sketch Palette.

3. On the Toolbar, click the **Sketch** tab > **Create** panel > **Polygon** drop-down > **Inscribed Polygon** .

4. Click the sketch origin.

5. Type-in 6 in the **Edge Number** box.

6. Move the pointer vertically upward. You will notice that a dotted trace line appears between the origin point and the pointer.

7. Click to create the polygon.

8. On the Toolbar, click the **Sketch** tab >

   Constraints panel > **Horizontal/Vertical** .

9. Select the vertices of the polygon, as shown.

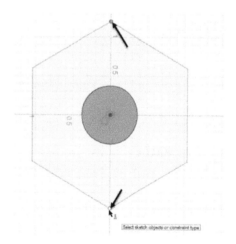

10. Activate the **Sketch Dimension** tool and create a dimension, as shown in a figure.

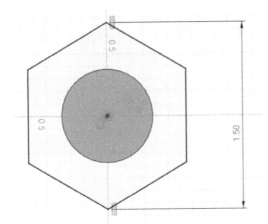

11. Click **Finish Sketch** on the Toolbar.
12. Activate the **Extrude** tool and click on the region enclosed by the sketch.
13. On the **Extrude** dialog, type-in -0.5 in the **Distance** box.
14. Select **Operation > Join**.
15. Click **OK**.

Adding Threads

1. On the Toolbar, click the **Solid** tab > **Create** panel > **Thread** .
2. Click on the round face of the model geometry.
3. On the **Thread** dialog, uncheck the **Full Length** option and type-in **1.5** in the **Length** box.
4. Check the **Modeled** option.
5. Select **Thread Type > ANSI Unified Screw Threads**.
6. Set **Size** to **0.75**.
7. Select **Designation > 3/4 -10 UNC**.
8. Select **Class > 2A**.
9. Select **Direction > Right hand**.

10. Click **OK** to add the thread.

11. Save and close the file.

TUTORIAL 7

In this tutorial, you create a plastic casing.

Creating the First Feature

1. Start Autodesk Fusion 360.
2. On the Toolbar, click the **Solid** tab > **Create** panel > **Create Sketch**.
3. Select the XY Plane.
4. Click the **Look At** icon on the Sketch Palette.
5. On the Toolbar, click the **Sketch** tab> **Create** panel > **Line**.
6. Click on the second quadrant, move the cursor horizontally toward the right, and then click to create a horizontal line, as shown.

7. On the Toolbar, click the **Sketch** tab > **Create**

panel > **Arc** drop-down > **3-Point Arc**.

8. Select the right endpoint of the horizontal line.
9. Move the cursor vertically downwards and click to define the second point.
10. Move the pointer towards the right and click on the horizontal axis line.

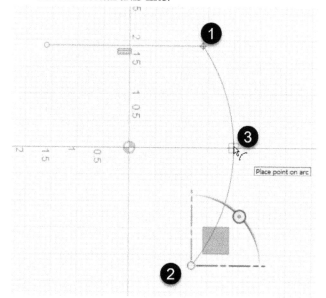

11. Likewise, create another three-point arc and horizontal line, as shown.

12. Create a vertical construction line from the origin point.

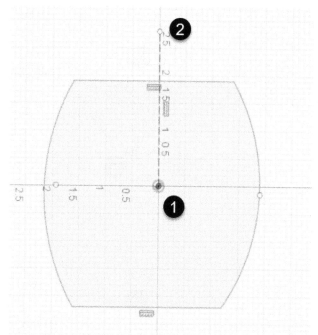

13. On the Toolbar, click the **Sketch** tab > **Constraints** panel > **Symmetry**.
14. Select the two arcs and the construction line.

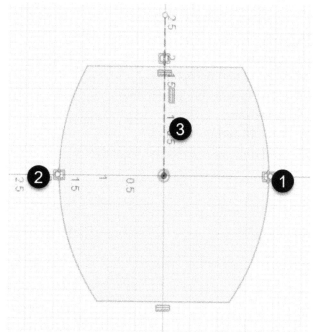

15. Likewise, create a horizontal construction line from the origin point, and then make the two horizontal lines symmetric about it.

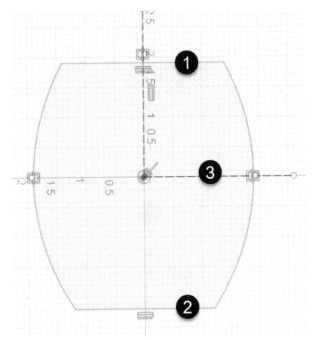

16. On the Toolbar, click the **Sketch** tab > **Constraints** panel > **Equal**.
17. Select the two horizontal lines.
18. On the Toolbar, click the **Sketch** tab > **Create** panel > **Sketch Dimension**.
19. Select any one of the arcs and place the dimension.
20. Type 30 and press Enter.
21. Select the two horizontal lines and place the dimension.
22. Type 20 and press Enter.
23. Add dimension to the horizontal line.

24. Click **Finish Sketch**.
25. Click the **Home** icon located at the top left corner of the ViewCube.
26. Click the **Solid** tab > **Create** panel > **Extrude** on

the Toolbar; the **Extrude** dialog appears.
27. Click on the region enclosed by the sketch.
28. Set the **Distance** to 3.15.
29. Set the **Taper Angle** value to -10.
30. Click the **OK** button.

Creating the Extruded surface

1. Click the **Solid** tab > **Create** panel > **Create Sketch** on the Toolbar, and then select the YZ Plane.

2. Click the **Look At** icon on the Sketch Palette.
3. Check the **Slice** option on the **Sketch Palette**.
4. Click the **Sketch** tab > **Create** panel > **Spline** > **Fit Point Spline** on the Toolbar.
5. Create a spline, as shown in figure (See Chapter 5, Tutorial 4, Creating the First Section and Rails section).

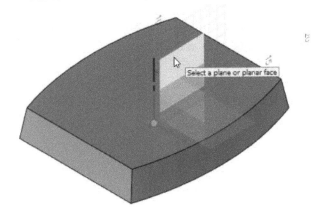

6. Apply dimensions to the spline, as shown below.

Adding a dimension between two points of a spline locks the distance between the two points.

7. Click **Finish Sketch**.
8. On the Toolbar, click the **Surface** tab.
9. On the **Surface** tab of the Toolbar, click **Create > Extrude**.

10. Select the sketch.
11. Select **Direction > Symmetric**.
12. Set the **Measurement** to **Whole Length** .
13. Type 17 in the **Distance** box.
14. Select **Operation > New Body**.
15. Click **OK**.

Replacing the top face of the model with the surface

1. On the **Solid** tab of the Toolbar, click **Modify** panel > **Replace Face**.

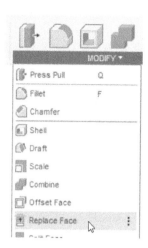

Now, you need to select the face to be replaced.

2. Select the top face of the model.

Next, you need to select the target face or surface.

3. Click the **Select** button next to the **Target Faces** option on the dialog.
4. Select the extruded surface.
5. Click **OK** to replace the top face with a surface.

6. Hide the extruded surface by clicking the right mouse button on it and then selecting **Show/Hide**.

Creating a fillet

1. On the **Solid** tab of the Toolbar, click **Modify > Fillet**.
2. Click on the two edges of the model, as shown.

3. Select **Radius Type > Constant Radius**.
4. Type **1.5** in the **Radius** box.
5. Click **OK**.

Creating a Variable Radius fillet

1. On the **Solid** tab of the Toolbar, click **Modify >**

Fillet.
2. On the **Fillet** dialog, check the **Tangent Chain** option.
3. Select the curved edge on the model; the preview of the fillet appears.

4. Select **Radius Type > Variable Radius**.
5. Select a point on the fillet, as shown in the figure.

6. Select another point on the fillet, as shown in the figure.

7. Click on the arrow displayed on the endpoint of the edge.
8. Type 0.6 in the **Radius** box.
9. Likewise, change the radius and position values at the other points, as shown.

You can also specify the fillet continuity type.

7.   Select the **Curvature (G2)** option **Continuity** drop-down located next to the **Radius** box.
8.   Click **OK** to create the variable fillet.

9.   Likewise, create another variable radius fillet on the other side.

Shelling the Model

1.   On the Toolbar, click the **Solid** tab > **Modify** panel > **Shell**; the **Shell** dialog appears.
2.   Select **Direction > Inside**.
3.   Rotate the model and select the bottom face.
4.   Type **0.2** in the **Inside Thickness** box.

5.   Click **OK**.
6.   Save and close the model.

TUTORIAL 8

In this tutorial, you construct a patterned cylindrical shell.

Constructing a cylindrical shell

1.   Start Autodesk Fusion 360.
2.   Create a sketch on the XY plane, as shown.

3.   Extrude the sketch up to 3.93 depth.

Adding a Slot

1. Activate the **Create Sketch** tool.
2. Select the XZ Plane.

3. Click the **Look At** icon on the **Sketch Palette**.
4. Check the **Slice** option on the **Sketch Palette**. The model is sliced using the sketching plane.
5. On the Toolbar, click the **Sketch** tab > **Create** panel > **Slot** drop-down > **Center to Center Slot**.

6. Click to define the first point of the slot.
7. Move the pointer up and click to define the second point.
8. Move the pointer outward and click to create a slot.

9. Apply the **Vertical constraint** between the Center point of the slot and the origin point.
10. Add dimensions to the slot.

11. Click **Finish Sketch**.
12. Click the **Home** icon next to the ViewCube.
13. On the Toolbar, click the **Solid** tab > **Create** panel > **Extrude**.
14. Click on the region enclosed by the sketch.
15. On the **Extrude** dialog, select **Extent** > **All**.
16. Make sure that the arrow on the feature points in the forward direction.

17. Select **Operation** > **Cut** from the dialog.
18. Click **OK**.

Constructing the Rectangular pattern

1. On the Toolbar, click the **Solid** tab > **Create** > **Pattern** > **Rectangular Pattern** .
2. On the **Rectangular Pattern** dialog, select **Pattern Type** > **Features**.

3. Click on the **Extrude2** feature in the Timeline.

4. On the **Rectangular Pattern** dialog, click the **Select** button next to the **Directions** option.
5. Select the Z Axis from the coordinate system.

6. On the dialog, select the **Spacing** option from the **Distance Type** drop-down.
7. Type **6** in the **Quantity** box.
8. Type **0.629** in the **Distance** box.
9. Click **OK**.

Constructing the Circular pattern

1. On the Toolbar, click the **Solid** tab > **Create**

panel > **Pattern** > **Circular Pattern** .

2. On the **Circular Pattern** dialog, select **Pattern Type** > **Features**.

3. In the timeline, click on the **R-Pattern1** and the **Extrude2** features.

4. On the **Circular Pattern** dialog, click the **Select** button next to the **Axis** option and select the cylindrical face of the model.

5. Select **Type** > **Full**.

6. Type-in **12** in the **Quantity** box.

7. Click **OK** to make the circular pattern.

11. Save and close the model.

Chapter 7: Top-Down Assembly and Joints

In this chapter, you will learn to

- Create a top-down assembly
- Create assembly joints

TUTORIAL 1

In this tutorial, you will create the model shown in the figure. You use the top-down assembly approach to create this model.

Creating a component in the Assembly

In a top-down assembly approach, you create components of an assembly directly in the assembly by using the **Create** tool.

1. Click the **Save** icon on the Application Bar.
2. Type Ch7_tut1 in the Name box on the Save dialog.
3. Click Save.
4. Click **New Component** on the **Assemble** panel of the Toolbar. The **New Component** dialog appears.

5. Select the **Empty Component** option.
6. Enter **Base** in the **Name** field.
7. Check the **Activate** option.
8. Click **OK**.
9. Click **Solid > Create > Create Sketch** on the Toolbar.
10. Select the **XY Plane**.
11. Create a sketch, as shown below.

12. Click **Finish Sketch**.
13. Click **Solid > Create > Extrude** on the Toolbar and extrude the sketch up to 1.5 in.

14. Start a sketch on the top face and draw a circle of **2** in diameter.

15. Click **Finish Sketch.**
16. Extrude the sketch up to 3.75 inches distance.

17. Create a counterbore hole on the second feature (See Chapter 6, Tutorial 1, Create a Counterbore Hole section). The following figure shows the dimensions of the counterbore hole.

18. Start a new sketch on the top face of the first feature.
19. Create a 3.5 diameter circle with the

Construction button pressed on the Sketch Palette.

20. On the Toolbar, click **Sketch > Create** drop-down **> Point**.
21. Place a point on the circle.
22. On the Toolbar, click **Sketch > Constraints > Horizontal/Vertical**.
23. Select the sketch origin and the point.

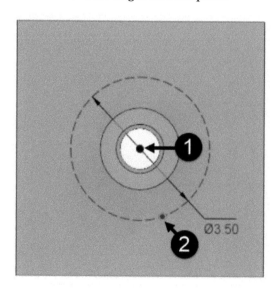

24. Click **Finish Sketch**.
25. On the Toolbar, click **Solid > Create > Hole**.
26. Select the sketch point.
27. On the **Hole** dialog, specify the settings, as shown.

28. Click **OK** to create the hole.

29. Create a circular pattern of the hole (See Chapter 6, Tutorial 1, Create a Circular Pattern).

30. In the **Browser**, right click on **Ch7_tut1**, and then select **Activate**; the assembly is activated.

Creating the Second Component of the Assembly

1. Click **Solid > Assemble > New Component** on the Toolbar; the **New Component** dialog appears.

2. Enter **Spacer** in the **Name** field.

3. Check the **Activate** option.

4. Click **OK**.

5. Click **Solid > Create > Create Sketch** on the Toolbar.

6. Select the top face of the Base.

7. On the Toolbar, click **Sketch > Create** drop-down **> Project/Include > Project** and select the circular edges of the Base.

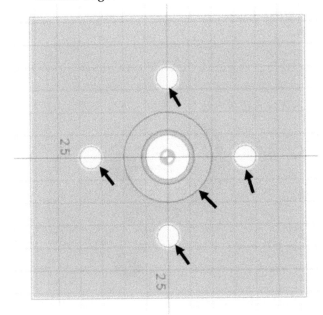

8. Click **OK**.

9. Draw a circle of 4.5 in diameter.

10. Click **Finish Sketch**.
11. Extrude the sketch up to 1.5 in.

6. Draw a sketch, as shown in the figure.

12. In the Browser, right click on Ch7_tut1 and select **Activate**.

Creating the third Component of the Assembly

1. Click **Solid > Assemble > New Component** on the Toolbar; the **New Component** dialog appears.
2. Enter **Shoulder Screw** in the **Name** field.
3. Check **Activate** option.
4. Click **OK**.
5. Start a sketch on the YZ Plane.

7. Click **Finish Sketch**.
8. Activate the **Revolve** tool and revolve the sketch.

9. On the Toolbar, click **Solid > Modify** drop-down > **Chamfer**.

10. Chamfer the edges, as shown in the figure. The Chamfer **Distance** is 0.06 in.

11. Activate the **Fillet** tool and fillet the edges, as shown in the figure. The fillet radius is 0.02 in.

12. Right-click on **Ch7_tut1** in the **Browser**, and then select **Activate**.

Create the Bolt

1. On the Toolbar, click **Solid > Assemble > New Component**.
2. On the **New Component** dialog, select the **Empty Component** option.
3. Type **Bolt** in the **Name** box.
4. Select the **Activate** option.
5. Click **OK**.
6. On the Toolbar, click **Solid > Create > Create Sketch**.
7. Click on the top face of the spacer.
8. On the Toolbar, click **Solid > Create** drop-down > **Project/Include > Project**.
9. Click on the hole edge.

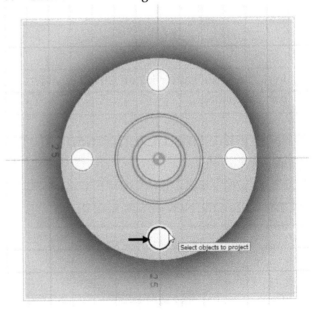

10. Click **OK**.
11. Click **Finish Sketch**.
12. On the Toolbar, click **Solid > Create > Extrude**.
13. Click on the region enclosed by the sketch.
14. Type -3.5 in the **Distance** box and click **OK**.

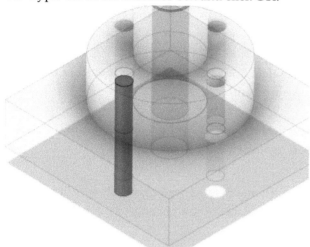

15. On the Toolbar, click **Solid > Create** drop-down
    > **Create Sketch**.
16. Click on the top face of the extruded feature.
17. Create a polygon, as shown in the figure.

18. Click **Finish Sketch**.
19. Extrude the sketch up to 0.25 inches distance.

20. Activate the assembly.

Patterning components in an assembly

1. On the Toolbar, click **Solid > Create** drop-down
   > **Pattern > Circular Pattern**.
2. Select **Pattern Type > Components**.
3. Select the **Bolt** from the Browser.

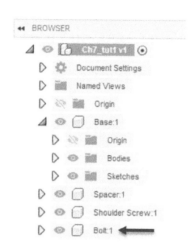

4. On the **Circular Pattern** dialog, click the **Select** button next to the **Axis** option.
5. Click on the large cylindrical face of the Spacer to define the axis of the circular pattern.
6. On the dialog, type-in 4 in the **Quantity** box
7. Select **Type > Full**.
8. Click **OK** to pattern the bolt.

Creating a Rigid Group

1. In the Browser, right click on the **Base** component, and then select **Ground**.

2. On the Toolbar, click **Solid > Assemble > Rigid Group**.

3. Select all the components one-by-one.
4. Click **OK** to create the rigid group.

Using the Measure tool

The **Measure** tool helps you to measure the size and position of the model. You can measure the various parameters of the model, such as length, angle, and radius.

1. On the Toolbar, click **Solid > Inspect > Measure** ; the **Measure** dialog appears on the screen.

The **Measure** dialog has three selection filters (shown from left to right): **Select Face/Edge/Vertex**, **Select Body**, and **Select Component**.

The **Select Face/Edge/Vertex** filter allows you to select only the faces, edges, and vertices of the model.

The **Select Body** filter allows you to select a body for measurement.

The **Select Component** filter allows you to select the part geometry and assemblies.

2. Click the **Select Face/Edge/Vertex** filter, and then select the straight edge, as shown.

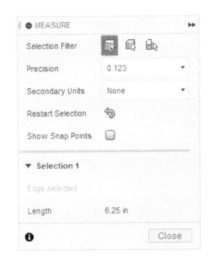

The length of the selected edge is displayed on the **Measure** dialog.

3. Select the round face, as shown; the Measure window displays results.

Face selected

The **Measure** dialog displays the results of the first and second selections separately. In addition to that, the distance between the two selected entities is displayed.

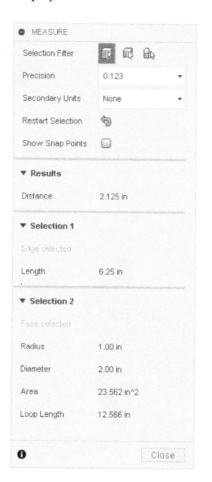

4. Close the **Measure** dialog.
5. Save and close the assembly and its parts.

TUTORIAL 2

In this tutorial, you create a slider-crank mechanism by applying Joints.

1. Create the **Slider Crank Assembly** folder inside the project folder.
2. Download the part files of the assembly by reaching us at online.books999@gmail.com.
3. Click the **Show Data Panel** icon on the top left corner of the window.
4. Click the **Upload** button on the **Data** panel.
5. On the **Upload** dialog, set the **Location** to **Autodesk Fusion 360 Basics Tutorial > master > Slider Crank Assembly**.
6. Click the **Select Files** button.
7. Select the downloaded part files, and then click **Open**.
8. Click **Upload** on the **Upload** dialog.
9. Click **Close** on the **Job Status** dialog.
10. Start a new assembly file.

Inserting the Components into the Design

1. On the Application Bar, click the Save icon.
2. Type Slider Crank Assembly in the Name box on the Save dialog.
3. Click Save.

4. To insert the base component, click the Show Data Panel icon.
5. Right click on the Base file in the Data panel, and then select **Insert into Current Design**.
6. Click **OK**.
7. In the **Browser**, right click on the Base component, and then select **Ground**.
8. Insert the remaining components into the design.

Creating the Slider Joint

1. Click **Solid > Assemble > Joint** on the Toolbar; the **Joint** dialog appears.

2. Click the **Motion** tab.
3. Set the **Type** to **Slider**.

4. Click the **Position** tab, and then click **Mode > Simple** icon.
5. Click the **Select** button next to the **Snap** option.
6. Select the face on the Slider1, as shown below.

7. Select the face on the Base, as shown below; the two faces are aligned.

8. Type 180 in the **Angle** box.
9. On the dialog, click the **Motion** tab and select **Slide > Y Axis**.
10. Click the **Animate** ▶ icon; the slider slides along with the slot.

Before defining the joint limits, you need to know the distance between the center of Slider 1 and anyone of the limiting faces

11. Click the **Stop** ■ icon.
12. Click **OK**.

1. On the Toolbar, click **Inspect > Measure**.
2. Select the two faces, as shown.

Editing the Joint Limits

You have noticed that the slider slides beyond the base component. You need to restrict the motion of the slider between the two faces, as shown.

3. In the **Measure** dialog, click on the **Minimum Distance** value in the **Results** section; the value is copied to the clipboard.

4. Close the **Measure** dialog.
5. In the Browser, expand the **Joints** folder, right click on the **Slider 1** joint, and then select **Edit Joint Limits**.

6. Check the **Maximum** option.
7. Select the value in the **Maximum** box.
8. Press **CTRL+V** to paste the maximum distance value in the box.
9. Check the **Minimum** box.
10. Type -1.51 in the **Minimum** box.

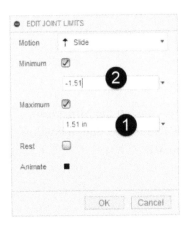

11. Click **OK**.
12. Right click on the Slider 1 joint in the Browser and then select **Animate Joint**; the slider joint is animated. Notice that the slider moves between the end faces of the Base component.
13. Press **Esc** to stop the animation.

Creating Second Slider Joint

1. Click the corner of the ViewCube, as shown; the orientation of the design is changed.

2. Click **Assemble > Joint** on the Toolbar.
3. Click the **Motion** tab.
4. Set the **Type** to **Slider**.
5. Click the **Position** tab, and then click **Mode > Simple** icon.
6. Click the **Select** button next to the **Snap** option.
7. Select the face on the Slider2, as shown below.

8. Select the right edge of the top face of the ViewCube; the orientation of the design changes.

9. Click the **Fit** icon on the Navigation Bar
10. Select the face on the Slider1, as shown below.
11. On the dialog, click the **Motion** tab and select **Slide > X Axis**.
12. Click **OK**.

Click at this location

Creating the Revolute Joint

1. Click **Solid > Assemble > Joint** on the Toolbar.
2. Click the **Motion** tab.
3. Set **Type** to **Revolute**.

4. Click the **Position** tab, and then click **Mode > Simple** icon.
5. Click the **Select** button next to the **Snap** option.
6. Select the circular edge of the arm, as shown below.

7. Select the circular edge of the Slider2.

13. Click the **Motion** tab.
14. Select **Rotate > Z-Axis**.
15. Click **OK.**

Creating the Rigid Joint

1. Click the **Home** icon next to the ViewCube.
2. Click on the round face of the Arm and drag it towards left; the arm is revolved.

Face to drag

3. Click **Assemble > Joint** on the Toolbar.
4. Click the **Capture Position** button on the **Fusion 360** dialog.

5. Click the **Motion** tab.
6. Set the **Type** to **Rigid** .
7. Click the **Position** tab, and then click **Mode > Simple** icon.
8. Click the **Select** button next to the **Snap** option.
9. Select the top face on the pin.

Select location on component to move

10. Click on the corner point of the **ViewCube**, as shown.

11. Select the circular face of the arm.

Select location on second component

12. Click the **Flip** icon, if the pin is displayed on the opposite side.
13. Click **OK**.

Adding more assembly joints

1. Create another revolute joint between the Pin and the Pivot.

Next, you need to fix the Pivot.

2. On the Toolbar, click **Solid > Modify > Align**.

3. On the **Align** dialog, select **Object > Component**.

4. Select the bottom faces of the Pivot and Base.

5. Check the **Capture Position** option.
6. Click **OK**.
7. On the Toolbar, click **Solid > Modify > Align**.
8. On the **Align** dialog, select **Object > Component**.
9. In the Browser, expand the **Origin** folder and select the XZ plane.

10. In the Browser, expand the Pivot folder, and then expand the **Origin** folder under it.
11. Select the XZ Plane of the Pivot.
12. Check the **Capture Position** option, and then click **OK**.
13. In the Browser, right click on the Pivot component, and then select Ground; the component is grounded.

Creating Motion Links

1. On the Toolbar, click **Solid > Assemble > Motion Link**.

2. Click **Capture Position**.

3. Expand the **Joints** folder in the Browser and then select the two Revolute joints.

4. Check the **Reverse** option.
5. Click **OK**.
6. Right click on any one of the Revolute joints, and then select **Animate Model**; the model is animated.

7. Press Esc to stop the animation.
8. Save and close the assembly.

TUTORIAL 3

In this tutorial, you create the Ball Bearing assembly.

Creating the Outer Ring

1. Create a new project with the name **Ball Bearings** (See Chapter 2, Tutorial 1, Creating New Project section to learn how to create a new project).
2. Click **File > New Design** on the Application bar.
3. Click **Solid** tab **> Create** panel **> Create Sketch** on the Toolbar, and select the XY Plane.

4. Click the **Look At** icon on the Sketch Palette.
5. Click **Sketch** contextual tab **> Create** panel **> 2-Point Rectangle** on the Toolbar.
6. Draw a rectangle, as shown.

7. Click **Create > Arc > 3-Point Arc** on the **Sketch** contextual tab of the Toolbar.
8. Create an arc, as shown in the figure.

9. Click the **Sketch** contextual tab **> Constraints > Horizontal/Vertical** and select the centerpoint of the arc and the origin point; the centerpoint of the arc and origin are aligned vertically.

Selections

139

10. On the **Sketch** contextual tab of the Toolbar, expand the **Modify** panel and click the **Trim** icon.

11. Select the portion between the arc, as shown.

12. Click **Sketch** contextual tab > **Constriants** panel > **Equal** on the toolbar.

13. Select the horizontal lines, as shown.

14. Click **Sketch** contextual tab > **Create** panel > **Sketch Dimension** on the toolbar and apply dimensions as shown.

15. Click **Finish Sketch** on the Toolbar.

16. Click the **Home** icon on the top left corner of the ViewCube.

17. Click **Solid** tab > **Create** > **Revolve** on the Toolbar and select the enclosed region of the sketch, as shown.

18. On the **Revolve** dialog, click on the **Select** button next to **Axis**.

19. Select the **X** axis from the graphics window; the preview of the revolved feature appears.

X axis

20. Select **Type** > **Full** from the **Revolve** dialog.

21. Click **OK** on the dialog.

22. Click **Modify** > **Fillet** on the **Solid** tab of the Toolbar.

23. Select the outer circular edges of the revolved feature, as shown.

24. Select **Radius Type > Constant Radius**.
25. Enter 0.08 in the **Radius** box and click **OK**.
26. Click **Save** on the Application bar and enter **Outer Ring** in the **Name** field.
27. Click **Save** on the **Save** dialog to save the design file.
28. Close the design file.

Creating the Inner Ring

1. Click **File > New Design** on the Toolbar.
2. On the Toolbar, click **Sketch** contextual tab > **Create** panel > **Create Sketch** and select the XY Plane.
3. Create a sketch and add dimensions to the sketch, as shown.

4. Click **Finish Sketch** on the Toolbar.
5. Click the **Home** icon located at the top left corner of the ViewCube.
6. Click **Create** panel > **Revolve** on the **Solid** tab of the Toolbar and select the enclosed region of the sketch, as shown.

7. On the **Revolve** dialog, click the **Select** button next to **Axis**.
8. Select the **X** axis from the graphics window; the preview of the revolved feature appears.
9. Select **Type > Full** from the **Revolve** dialog.
10. Click **OK** on the dialog.

11. Click **Save** on the Application bar and enter **Inner Ring** in the **Name** field.
12. Click **Save** on the **Save** dialog.
13. Close the design file.

Creating the Ball

1. Click **File > New Design** on the Application bar.

2. Click **Create** panel > **Sphere** on the **Solid** tab of the Toolbar.

3. Select the XY Plane.
4. Select the origin point to define the center point of the sphere.
5. Type **0.944** in the **Diameter** box.

6. Click **OK** on the **Sphere** dialog.

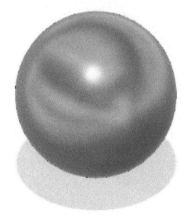

7. Click **Save** on the **Application bar** and enter **Ball** in the **Name** field
8. Click **Save**.
9. Close the design file.

Creating Cage

1. Click **File > New Design** on the Application bar.
2. Click the **Solid** tab > **Create** panel > **Create Sketch** and select the **XY** Plane.

3. Click the **Sketch** tab > **Create** panel drop-down > **Circle** > **Center Diameter Circle**.
4. Click on the origin point to define the center point of the circle and move the pointer outward.
5. Click to create a circle.
6. Likewise, create another circle and apply dimensions, as shown.

7. Click **Finish Sketch** on the Toolbar.
8. Click **Solid** tab > **Create** panel > **Extrude** on the Toolbar.
9. Click on the region enclosed by the outer and inner circle.
10. Select **Extent > Distance** and enter **0.62** in the **Distance** box.
11. Select **Direction > Symmetric**.
12. Select **Measurement > Whole Length** ⊟.

13. Click **OK** on the dialog.

14. Click **Solid** tab **> Create** panel **> Create Sketch** on the Toolbar.
15. Click on the top face of the extruded face.
16. Create the sketch, as shown.

17. Click **Finish Sketch** on the Toolbar.
18. Click the **Home** icon located at the top left corner of the ViewCube.
19. Click **Solid** tab **> Create** panel **> Revolve** on the Toolbar and click on the regions enclosed by the sketch.
20. On the **Revolve** dialog, click the **Select** button next to **Axis** and select the vertical line of the sketch, as shown.

21. Select **Type > Full** and **Operation > Cut** from the dialog.

22. Click **OK** to create the *Revolve Cut* feature.

23. Click the **Sketch** tab **> Modify** panel **> Fillet** on the Toolbar and select the two edges of the *Revolve Cut* feature, as shown.

24. On the dialog, select **Radius Type > Constant Radius** and type-in 0.08 in the **Radius** box.
25. Click **OK** on the dialog.

26. Click **Create** panel **> Pattern** drop-down **> Circular Pattern** on the **Solid** tab of the Toolbar.

27. On the **Circular** dialog, select **Pattern Type > Features** and select the **Revolve** and **Fillet** feature from the **Timeline**.

28. Click the **Select** button next to **Axis**.

29. Expand the **Origin** folder of the **Browser** window and select the **Z axis**.

30. Select **Type > Full** and type-in 8 in the **Quantity** box.

31. Click **OK** to create the pattern.

32. Click **Modify** panel **> Shell** on the **Solid** tab of the Toolbar

33. Select the outer face, inner face, and the bottom face of the part model.

34. Select **Direction > Inside** on the dialog and type-in **0.059** in the **Inside Thickness** box.

35. Click **OK** to create the *Shell* feature.

36. Click **Solid** tab **> Create** panel **> Create Sketch** on the Toolbar and select the top face of the part model, as shown.

37. Click the **Look At** icon on the Sketch Palette.

38. On the **Sketch Palette**, click **Options > Construction** icon.

39. Click **Sketch** tab **> Create** panel **> Center Diameter Circle** on the Toolbar.

40. Click on the origin point to define the center point of the sketch and move the pointer outward.

41. Type-in **3.54** in the distance box and click to create the circle.

42. Activate the **Line** command and click on the origin point and move the pointer onto the circle and click to create an inclined line.

43. Likewise, create another line, as shown.

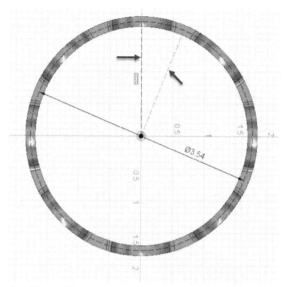

44. Press Esc.
45. Deselect the **Construction** icon on the **Sketch Palette**.
46. Create a circle on the endpoint of the construction line, as shown.

47. Activate the **Sketch Dimension** command and add dimensions to the sketch, as shown.

48. Click **Finish Sketch** on the Toolbar.
49. Click the **Home** icon located at the top left corner of the ViewCube.
50. Click **Solid** tab > **Create** panel > **Extrude** on the Toolbar.
51. Click on the region enclosed by the sketch.
52. Select **Operation** > **Cut** on the **Extrude** dialog.
53. Select **Extents** > **All** and click the **Flip** icon on the dialog.
54. Click **OK** to create the *Extruded Cut* feature.
55. Click **Solid** tab > **Create** panel > **Pattern** drop-down > **Circular pattern** on the Toolbar.
56. On the **Circular Pattern** dialog, select **Pattern Type** > **Features** and select the *Extruded Cut* feature from the part model.
57. Click the **Select** button next to **Axis** and select the **Z-axis**.

58. On the dialog, select **Type** > **Full** and type-in **8** in the **Quantity** box.
59. Click **OK** to create the circular pattern.

60. Click **Save** on the **Application bar** and enter Cage in the **Name** field.
61. Click **Save**.
62. Close the design file.

Assembling all the Part Models

1. Click **Save** on the **Application bar** and enter **Ball Bearing Assembly** in the **Name** field and click **Save**.
2. Click **Show Data Panel** on the **Application bar**.
3. Select the **Outer Ring** file.
4. Right-click and select **Insert into Current Design**.
5. Click **OK** on the **Move/Copy** dialog.
6. In the **Browser** window, right-click on the **Outer Ring** and click **Ground**.

10. Likewise, insert the **Ball** into the Design file.
11. Click **OK** on the **Move/Copy** dialog.

7. Select the **Inner Ring** from the **Data** Panel.
8. Right-click and select **Insert into Current Design**.
9. Click **OK** on the **Move/Copy** dialog.

12. On the Toolbar, click the **Joint** icon on the **Assemble** panel.
13. Select the circular edges of the inner and outer ring.
14. Click the **Motion** tab.
15. Select **Type > Revolute** from the **Joint** dialog.
16. Select **Rotate > Z Axis**.

146

Selections

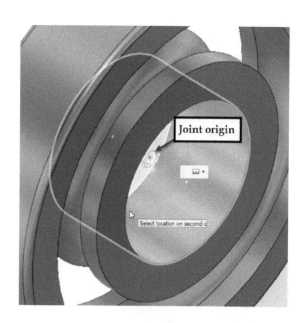

Joint origin

Select location on second c

17. Click **OK**.
18. On the Toolbar, click the **Joint** icon on the **Assemble** panel.
19. Select the Ball.

Select location on component to move

20. Move the pointer on the inner cylindrical face of the Inner ring.
21. Click when the Joint origin located at the midpoint is highlighted.

22. On the **Joint** dialog, type 1.787 in the **Offset X** box.

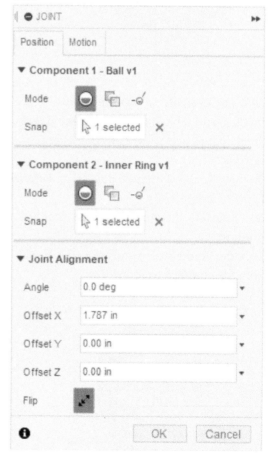

23. Click the **Motion** tab, and then select **Type > Revolute**.
24. Select **Rotate > Z Axis**.

25. Click **OK** to create the **Revolute** joint.
26. On the **Solid** tab of the toolbar, expand the **Create** panel, and select **Pattern > Circular Pattern**.
27. On the **Circular Pattern** dialog, select **Pattern Type > Components**.
28. Select the Ball component from the graphics window.
29. Click the **Select** button and select the X axis from the graphics window.

30. Select **Type > Full**.
31. Type 8 in the **Quantity** box.
32. Click **OK**.

33. In the Browser, turn off the visibility icon next to the Outer Ring body.

34. Select the **Cage** from the **Data** panel.
35. Right-click and select **Insert into Current Design**.
36. Press and hold the left mouse button on the Rotation handle, and then drag the pointer.

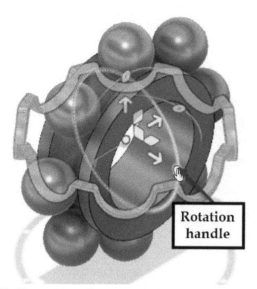

Rotation handle

37. Type **-90** in the **Y Angle** box.
38. Click **OK** on the **Move/Copy** dialog.

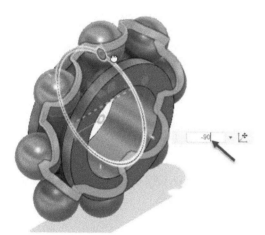

39. On the Toolbar, click the **Joint** icon on the **Assemble** panel.
40. Select the circular face of the cage, as shown.

41. Select the Ball.

42. Click the **Motion** tab.
43. Select **Type > Ball** from the **Joint** dialog.
44. Click **OK**.

45. On the **Solid** tab of the toolbar, expand the **Create** panel, and click the **Mirror** icon.
46. Select **Pattern Type > Components** from the **Mirror** dialog.
47. Select the cage from the graphics window.
48. Select the **Select** button next to the **Mirror Plane** option.
49. Select the YZ Plane from the graphics window.

50. Click **OK** on the **Mirror** dialog.

51. On the toolbar, expand the **Assemble** panel and click the **Rigid Group** icon.
52. Select all ball components and cage.

53. Click **Yes** on the **Fusion 360** message box.
54. Select the mirrored cage.

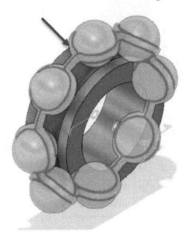

55. Click **OK**; the rigid group is created.

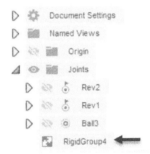

56. Click and drag one of the balls; the entire rigid group moves.
57. In the Browser, turn ON the visibility icon next to the Outer Ring body.

58. Click **Save** on the Application Bar.
59. Close the design file.

Chapter 8: Dimensions and Annotations

In this chapter, you will learn to

- Create Centerlines and Centered Pattern
- Edit Hatch Pattern
- Apply Dimensions
- Place Hole callouts
- Place Leader Text
- Place Datum Feature
- Place Feature control frame
- Place Surface texture symbol
- Modify the Title Block Information

TUTORIAL 1

In this tutorial, you create the drawing shown below.

Starting a New Drawing File

1. Click on the **Show Data Panel** icon on the Application Bar.
2. On the **Data** panel, double-click on the **Ch6_tut1** file to open it.
3. Close the **Data** panel.
4. To start a new drawing, click the **File > New Drawing > From Design** on the Application Bar.

5. On the **Create Drawing** dialog, uncheck the **Full Assembly** option.
6. Select the body from the graphics window.
7. Select **Template > From Scratch**.
8. Select **Standard > ASME**.
9. Select **Units > in**.
10. Select **Sheet Size > A (8.5in x 11in)**.
11. Click **OK**.
12. Set the **Scale** to 2:1.
13. Select **Orientation > Front**.
14. Set the **Style** to **Visible Edges**.
15. Place the view on the right side on the drawing sheet.

16. Click **OK**.
17. Click **Drawing Views > Section View** on the Toolbar.
18. Select the front view.

19. Draw the section line on the front view.

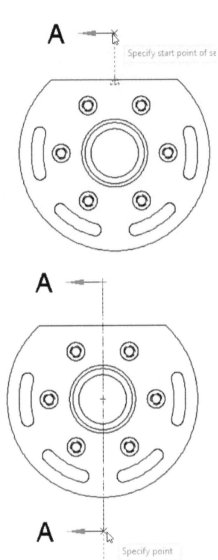

20. Right-click and select **Continue**.
21. Place the section view on the left side.
22. Click **OK**.

SECTION A-A
SCALE 2:1

Creating Centerlines and Centered Patterns

1. Click **Geometry > Centerline** on the Toolbar.

2. Select the parallel lines on the section view, as shown below; the centerline is created.

Lines to select

3. Right click and select **OK**.
4. Click **Geometry > Center Mark** on the Toolbar.

5. Select the circle located at the center.

6. On the Toolbar, click **Geometry > Center Mark Pattern** .
7. Select the center point of any one of the counterbored holes.

Edge to select

8. Check the **Auto-complete** and **Full PCD** options.
9. Click **OK**.
10. Likewise, create another centered pattern on the curved slots.
11. Make sure that the **Full PCD** option is unchecked. Click **OK**.

Editing the Hatch Pattern

1. Double-click on the hatch pattern of the section view; the **Hatch** dialog appears.

You can select the required hatch pattern from the **Pattern** drop-down. Use the **Scale Factor** box to change the distance between the hatch lines. Type-in a value in the **Angle** box to the change the angle of the hatch lines.

2. Click **Close**.

Applying Dimensions

1. Click **Dimensions > Angular Dimension** on the Toolbar.
2. Select the centerlines of the slot, as shown.

3. Move the pointer toward left and click.

4. Create angular dimensions between the holes, and then between slots. To create the angular dimension between the slots, you need to create the angular dimension between the bolt circles.

154

5. Dimension the pitch circle radius of the slots.

6. With the **Dimension** tool active, select the horizontal line of the front view.
7. Right click and select **Quadrant**.
8. Select the lower quadrant point of the circular edge.

9. Place the dimension on the left side.

10. Activate the **Dimension** tool.
11. Select the counterbore hole and place the dimension, as shown below.

20. Click **Text > Leader** on the Toolbar.

12. Right click and select **OK**.
13. Double click on the diameter dimension.
14. Click before the dimension value.

21. Select the slot end, as shown below.

15. On the **Dimension** dialog, select **Insert Symbol > Counterbore**.
16. Click after the dimension value.

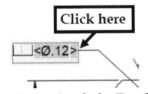

17. Select **Insert Symbol > Depth**.
18. Type **0.4** and click **Close** on the **Dimension** dialog.

22. Move the cursor away and click.
23. Enter the text shown below.

19. Add a pitch circle diameter to the counterbore holes.

24. Click **Close**.

Dimensions and Annotations

25. Double-click on the section label below the section view.
26. Select all the text.
27. On the **Text** dialog, set the **Height** to **0.12 in**. Click **Close**.
28. Click on the section label.
29. Select the square grip, move the pointer upward, and then place the label at the top.

30. Click **Dimension** on the **Dimensions** panel.
31. Select the vertical edge of the section view, as shown below.

32. Move the pointer toward the right and click to place the dimension.
33. Right click and select **OK**.
34. Double click on the dimension.
35. Click before the dimension.
36. On the **Dimension** dialog, expand the **Tolerance** section.
37. Select **Type > Symmetrical**.
38. Set the **Tolerance** value to **0.01**.

39. Click **Close**.

40. Likewise, create the other dimensions, as shown below.

Placing the Datum Identifier

1. Click **Symbols > Datum Identifier** on the Toolbar.

2. Select the edge of the section view, as shown below.

3. Move the cursor toward left and click.
4. Move the cursor downward and click.
5. Move the cursor toward left and click; the **Datum Identifier** dialog appears. Make sure that A is entered in the dialog.
6. Click **OK**.

7. Likewise, place a datum feature B, as shown below.

Placing the Feature Control Frame

1. Click **Symbols > Feature Control Frame** on the Toolbar.

2. Select the edge, as shown below.

3. Move the cursor horizontally toward the right and click.
4. Move the cursor downward and click to specify the location.
5. Right click and select **Continue**.
6. On the **Feature Control Frame** dialog, select the **Circular Runout** symbol from the **Geometric Symbol** section.

7. Enter 0.001 in the **First Tolerance** box and **A** in the **First Datum** box.
8. Click **OK**.

Placing the Surface Texture Symbols

1. Click **Symbols > Surface Texture** on the Toolbar.

2. Click on the inner cylindrical face of the hole, as shown below.

3. Specify the start point on the selected edge.
4. Move the pointer diagonally toward the right, and then click specify the location of the symbol.

5. Right-click and select **Continue**; the **Surface Texture** dialog appears.
6. Set the **Roughness Max** value to 63.
7. Click **OK**.

8. Apply the other annotations of the drawing.

9. Save the file.
10. To export the file to AutoCAD format, click **Output > Output DWG**.

11. Select **AutoCAD DWG** from the **Format** drop-down.
12. Click **OK**.
13. Click **Save**.
14. Close the file.

Chapter 9: Sheet Metal Modeling

Tutorial 1

In this tutorial, you will create a sheet metal model, as shown.

1. Start the **Autodesk Fusion 360** application.
2. Click **Modify** panel > **Sheet Metal Rules** on the **Sheet Metal** tab of the Toolbar.

3. Place the pointer on the **Aluminum (in)** material and click the **New Rule** icon.

4. On the **New Rule** dialog, type **Sample** in the name box.
5. Type **0.03** in the **Thickness** box.

6. Click **Save**.
7. Click **Close** on the **Sheet Metal Rules** dialog.
8. Click the **Create Sketch** icon on the **Create** panel of the **Sheet Metal** tab of the Toolbar.
9. Select the XY Plane.
10. Click the **2-Point Rectangle** icon on the **Create** panel of the **Sketch** toolbar.
11. Click the **Center Rectangle** icon on the Sketch Palette.

12. Create the rectangle and add dimensions to it, as shown.

9.00

13. Click **Finish Sketch** on the Toolbar.
14. Click the **Home** icon on the top left corner of the ViewCube.
15. On the **Sheet Metal** tab of the Toolbar, click the **Create** panel > **Flange**.

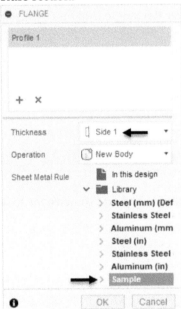

16. Click in the region enclosed by the sketch.
17. On the **Flange** dialog, select **Thickness > Side 1**.
18. Select the **Sample** option from the **Sheet Metal Rule** section.

19. Click **OK**.
20. Click the **Save** icon on the Application Bar.
21. Type **Ch9_tutorial 1** in the **Name** box.
22. Click the **Save** button.

23. On the **Sheet Metal** tab of the Toolbar, click the **Create** panel > **Flange**.
24. Click on the right and left edges of the sheet metal, as shown.

25. Type **4.5** in the **Height** box.
26. Select **Height Datum > Outer Faces**.
27. Select **Bend Position > Inside**.

28. Click **OK**.

162

29. On the **Sheet Metal** tab of the Toolbar, click the **Create** panel > **Flange**.
30. Select the edges of the model, as shown.

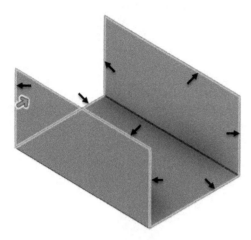

31. On the **Flange** dialog, type **0.5** in the **Height** box.
32. Click **OK**.

33. Click the **Create Sketch** icon on the **Create** panel of the **Sheet Metal** tab of the Toolbar.
34. Click on the front face.
35. Create a circle and add dimension to it.
36. Create a construction line connecting the origin point of the sketch and the top-left corner.
37. On the Toolbar, click the **Midpoint** icon on the **Constraints** panel.
38. Select the centerpoint of the circle.
39. Select the construction line; the circle is made coincident with the midpoint of the construction line.
40. Click **Finish Sketch**.

41. Click the **Extrude** icon on the **Create** panel of the **Sheet Metal** tab of the Toolbar.
42. Click in the region enclosed by the sketch.
43. Type **-0.03** in the **Distance** box.
44. Select the **Operation > Cut** and click **OK**.

45. Create a sketch on the front face of the model, as shown.

46. Create the extruded cut feature, as shown.

47. Select the extruded cut feature from the Timeline.
48. On the toolbar, click **Create** panel > **Pattern** drop-down > **Rectangular Pattern**.
49. On the **Rectangular Pattern** dialog, click the **Select** button next to the **Directions** button.
50. Select the horizontal edge of the flange, as shown.

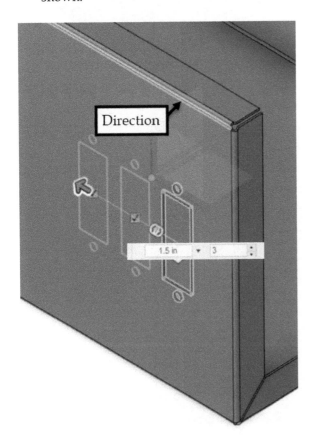

51. Type **3** and **1.5** in the **Quantity** and **Distance** boxes, respectively.
52. Click **OK** on the **Rectangular Pattern** dialog.
53. Click on the top-right corner of the ViewCube.

54. Click the **Create Sketch** icon on the **Create** panel of the **Sheet Metal** tab of the Toolbar.
55. Click on the flat face of the flange.
56. On the Toolbar, click **Create** panel > **Project**.
57. Select the circular edge of the Extruded cut feature.

58. Create the sketch, as shown.

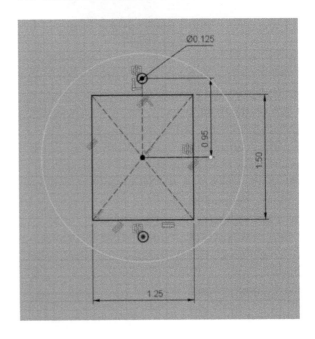

59. Create the extruded cut feature, as shown.

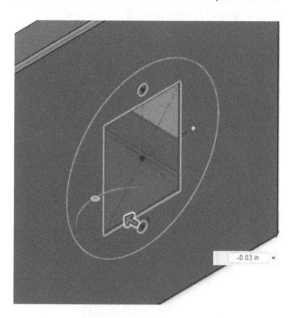

60. Click the **Home** icon on the top left corner of the ViewCube.
61. Click the **Create Sketch** icon on the **Create** panel of the **Sheet Metal** tab of the Toolbar.
62. Click on the flat face of the flange, as shown.

63. On the **Sketch** contextual bar, expand the **Create** panel and click the **Point** icon.
64. Create a point and add dimensions to it.

65. On the Toolbar, click **Solid** tab > **Create** panel > **Hole**.
66. Select the sketch point.

67. Select **Extents > All**.
68. Type **0.125** in the **Diameter** box.
69. Click **OK**.

70. Select the **Hole** feature from the Timeline.

71. On the **Sheet Metal** tab of the Toolbar, expand the **Create** panel, and click the Mirror icon.
72. On the **Mirror** dialog, click the **Select** button next to the **Mirror plane** option.
73. Select the XZ Plane from the graphics window.

74. Click **OK**.
75. On the **Sheet Metal** tab of Toolbar, expand the **Construct** panel, and click the **Midpoint** icon.

76. Select the top and bottom faces of the sheet metal model.
77. Click **OK**.

78. Press and hold the CTRL key and select the hole and the mirror feature from the Timeline.

79. On the Toolbar, click **Create** panel > **Mirror**.
80. Click the **Select** button next to the **Mirror Plane** option.
81. Select the midplane.

82. Click **OK**.
83. Click the **Create Sketch** icon on the **Create** panel of the **Sheet Metal** tab of the Toolbar.
84. Click on the bottom face.

85. Click the **Construction** icon on the Sketch Palette.
86. On the Toolbar, click **Create** panel > **Rectangle** > **Center Rectangle**.
87. Select the origin point of the sketch.
88. Move the pointer outward and click.
89. Add dimensions to the rectangle, as shown.

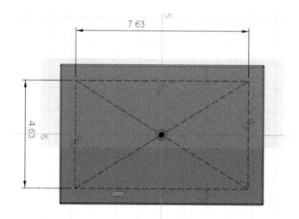

90. On the Toolbar, click **Create** panel > **Point**.
91. Select the corner points of the rectangle.

92. Click **Finish Sketch**.
93. On the Toolbar, click **Sheet Metal** tab > **Create** panel > **Hole**.
94. Select the corner points of the rectangle.
95. On the **Hole** dialog, select **Extents > All**.
96. Type 0.125 in the **Diameter** box and click **OK**.

97. Click the **Hide** icon next to the **Construction** folder in the Browser.

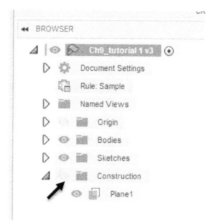

98. Click **Save** on the Application Bar.
99. Close the design file.

Tutorial 2

In this tutorial, you will insert the sheet metal part created in Tutorial 2 into an assembly. Next, you will create an enclosure.

1. Click the **Save** icon on the Application Bar.
2. Type **Ch9_tutorial2** in the **Name** box, and then click **Save**.
3. Click the **Show Data panel** icon on the top-left corner of the window.
4. Select **Ch9_tutorial1**.
5. Right-click and select **Insert into Current Design**.
6. Click **OK** on the **Move/Copy** dialog.
7. In the Browser, right-click on the Ch9_tutorial1 file.
8. Select **Ground** from the menu.

Creating a New Sheet Metal Component

1. On the **Sheet Metal** tab of the Toolbar, click **Create** panel > **New Component**.

2. On the **New Component** dialog, select the **Empty Component** option.
3. Type **Enclosure** in the **Name** box.
4. Check the **Activate** and **Sheet Metal Component** option.
5. Select **Sheet Metal Rule > Sample**.

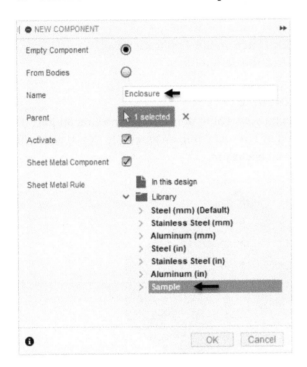

6. Click **OK**.
7. On the Toolbar, click **Create** panel > **Create Sketch**.
8. Click on the top face of the sheet metal file.

9. On the **Sketch** tab of the Toolbar, click **Create** panel > **Project/Include > Project**.

10. Zoom to the top left corner and select the edges, as shown.

11. Click **OK** on the **Project** dialog.
12. On the Toolbar, click **Create** panel > **Rectangle** > **Center Rectangle**.
13. Select the origin point of the sketch.
14. Move the pointer outward and click.
15. Expand the **Constraints** panel and click the **Collinear** icon.
16. Select the horizontal line of the rectangle and the horizontal projected edge.
17. Select the left vertical line of the rectangle and the vertical projected edge.

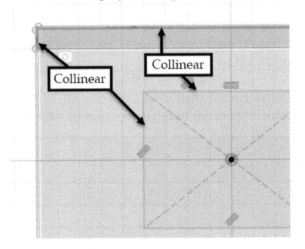

18. Click **Finish Sketch** on the Toolbar.
19. On the **Sheet Metal** tab of the Toolbar, click **Create** panel > **Flange**.
20. Click in the regions enclosed by the sketch.

21. Select **Thickness > Side 1**.
22. Click **OK**.

23. Click the **Flange** icon on the **Create** panel.
24. Select the bottom edge of the sheet metal.

25. Click the top left corner of the ViewCube.

26. Select the bottom edge, as shown.

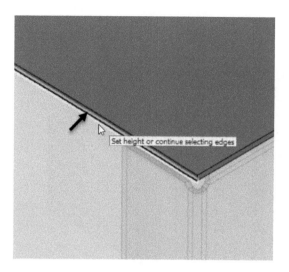

27. Type **4.53** in the **Height** box.
28. Select **Height Datum > Outer Faces**.
29. Select **Bend Position > Outside**.

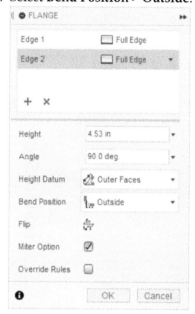

30. Click **OK**.
31. Create the flanges of the 0.5 height, as shown.

32. Click the top right corner of the ViewCube.

33. Create the flanges of 0.5 height.

34. Click the **Create Sketch** icon on the **Create** panel.
35. Click on the flat face of the sheet metal, as shown.

36. Expand the **Create** panel and click **Slot > Center Point Slot**.

37. Specify the three points of the slot, as shown.

38. Add dimensions to the sketch.

39. Click **Finish Sketch**.
40. Click the **Extrude** icon on the **Create** panel.
41. Click on the region enclosed by the sketch.
42. Type **-0.03** in the **Distance** box and click **OK**.

43. Click **Create Sketch** on the **Create** panel.
44. Select the outer face of the flange, as shown.

Select a plane or planar face

45. On the Navigate Bar, click **Display Settings > Visual Style > Wireframe**.

46. Expand the **Create** panel and click the **Project** icon.
47. Click on the circular edges of the holes.

48. Click **OK**.
49. Click **Finish Sketch**.
50. On the Navigate Bar, click **Display Settings > Visual Style > Shaded with Visible Edges Only**.
51. Click the **Extrude** icon on the **Create** panel.
52. Click on the region enclosed by the projected circles.
53. Type **-0.03** in the **Distance** box and click **OK**.

54. Press and hold the CTRL key and select the two extruded features from the Timeline, as shown.

55. Expand the **Create** panel and click the Mirror icon.
56. Click the **Select** button on the **Mirror Plane** option.
57. Select the YZ Plane from the graphics window.

58. Click **OK**.
59. Click the right mouse button on Ch9_tutorial2, and then select **Activate**.

Creating the Rubber Feet

1. Click the **New** icon on the Application Bar.
2. Click the **Create Sketch** icon on the **Create** panel of the **Solid** tab.
3. Select the XY Plane.
4. Create the sketch, as shown.

5. Click **Finish Sketch**.
6. Extrude the sketch up to 0.4 inches.

7. Click the **Create Sketch** icon on the **Create** panel of the **Solid** tab.
8. Select the XY Plane.

9. Create the sketch, as shown.

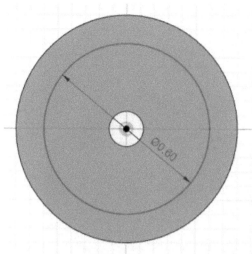

10. Click **Finish Sketch**.
11. Create an extruded cut feature of 0.1 inches.

12. Click **Save** on the Application Bar.
13. Type **Rubber Feet** in the **Name** box and click **Save**.

Inserting the Rubber Feet

1. Open the Ch9_tutorial2 file if not already open.
2. Click the **Show Data panel** icon on the top-left corner of the window.
3. Select **Rubber Feet**.
4. Right-click and select **Insert into Current Design**.

5. Click and drag the Y-axis of the manipulator, as shown.

6. Click **OK** on the **Move/Copy** dialog.
7. Click **Assemble > Joint** on the Toolbar.
8. Click the **Motion** tab.
9. Set the **Type** to **Rigid** .
10. Click the **Position** tab, and then click **Mode > Simple** icon.
11. Click the **Select** button next to the **Snap** option.
12. Select the top face of the rubber feet.

13. Click on the corner point of the **ViewCube**, as shown.

14. Select the circular edge of the hole, as shown.

173

15. Click **OK**.

16. Likewise, insert three more instances of the Rubber feet, and then create Rigid joints, as shown.

17. Click the **Home** icon on the top left corner of the ViewCube.
18. Click **Save** on the Application Bar.
19. Close the design file.